FATEFUL CHOICES

HEALTHY YOUTH FOR THE 21ST CENTURY

FRED M. HECHINGER

FATEFUL CHOICES

HEALTHY YOUTH FOR THE 21ST CENTURY

CARNEGIE COUNCIL ON ADOLESCENT DEVELOPMENT

CARNEGIE CORPORATION OF NEW YORK

Library of Congress Cataloging-in-Publication Data

Hechinger, Fred M.
    Fateful choices: healthy youth for the 21st century / Fred M. Hechinger.
        p.   cm.
    Includes bibliographical references and index.
    ISBN 0-9623154-2-7 (paperback)
    1. Youth — United States — Health and hygiene. I. Title.
RA564.5.H45 1992   92-4017
613'.0433'0973 — dc20   CIP

A hardback edition of *Fateful Choices: Healthy Youth for the 21st Century* is available from Hill and Wang, 19 Union Square West, New York, New York 10003.

FOR GRACE
AND OUR FORMER ADOLESCENTS
PAUL AND JOHN

CONTENTS

ACKNOWLEDGMENTS

T he idea of *Fateful Choices: Healthy Youth for the 21st Century* was born out of the concern and inspiration of David A. Hamburg, president of Carnegie Corporation of New York. His vision of a nation whose youth will be sound of body, mind, and spirit gave shape to this book. At all times, his guidance was crucial. Having first commissioned *Turning Points: Preparing American Youth for the 21st Century* as a guide to the reform of young adolescents' education in the middle schools, Hamburg envisioned *Fateful Choices* as a companion volume designed to deal with the healthy development of America's ten- to fifteen-year-olds.

The substance of this book was provided by the Carnegie Council on Adolescent Development. It commissioned key studies and reports, convened meetings of experts, and made available to me the wisdom of experienced researchers for guidance and review of the work while it was in progress. My thanks go to all the Council's members:

H. Keith H. Brodie	David E. Hayes-Bautista
Michael I. Cohen	David W. Hornbeck
Alonzo A. Crim	Daniel K. Inouye
Michael S. Dukakis	James M. Jeffords
William H. Gray III	Richard Jessor
Beatrix A. Hamburg	Helene L. Kaplan
David A. Hamburg	Nancy L. Kassebaum

Without the wisdom and leadership of Barbara D. Finberg, executive vice president of Carnegie Corporation, this project could not have been brought to fruition.

I am deeply indebted to the Council's executive director, Ruby Takanishi, for her genius at organization, for a constant flow of the latest research, and for keeping a sharp, critical eye on the developing manuscript.

For wise and patient advice, moral support, and continuing review, my gratitude goes to Vivien Stewart, chair of Carnegie Corporation's program on Education and Healthy Development of Children and Youth. The deep insights into adolescent health and behavior that Elena O. Nightingale, special adviser to the president of Carnegie Corporation, brought to the project were extraordinarily helpful.

Gloria Primm Brown, program officer, Carnegie Corporation; Jane M. Quinn, project director at the Council; and Michael H. Levine, program officer, Carnegie Corporation, all provided invaluable comments.

Along with his helpful counsel, Anthony W. Jackson, program officer, Carnegie Corporation, who brought his skills to the creation of *Turning Points*, gave me a model to aspire to.

It would be impossible to list the many names behind the research that made this book possible; their credits are contained in the references that make up the bibliography. My thanks go to each of them. One publication that should be singled out as an inspiration for much of the graphics that appear in this book is AMA *Profiles of Adolescent Health*, vol. 2, by Janet Gans, Margaret McManus, and Paul Newacheck.

I am especially indebted to Avery B. Russell, Carnegie Corporation's director of publications and program officer. Her experienced editorial hand gave the manuscript its essential final check. Sara Blackburn served as a highly professional editor whose work was eventually augmented most capably by Lurana M. Mayer.

Elizabeth Monroe expertly organized the bibliography, and Claire Sheridan diligently and ably helped in putting the final manuscript in shape.

Benjamin Tice Smith, photo editor of *Education Week*, provided many of the theme pictures, and Linda L. Schoff, administrative assistant to the Council, researched and coordinated the book's charts, graphs, and other pictorial embellishments. Katharine Beckman, office administrator for the Council, provided the vital liaison with Meadows & Wiser, the designers, and dealt with matters of copyright. All these functions helped immeasurably in creating the final product.

My special appreciation extends to Nidia Marti, administrative assistant, Carnegie Corporation, for the skill and devotion in her day-to-day assistance to me in moving this project from start to completion.

Finally, as in all my work, I owe unending gratitude to my wife, Grace, for her invaluable counsel and steady encouragement.

F.M.H.

t is a privilege to introduce a book that will do so much to improve the lives of so many for so long a time. In these pages, important challenges during the adolescent years are addressed in a most thoughtful, well-informed, and constructive way. These problems have great social and economic significance for the future of our society and have been too long neglected. Yet, this book shows that much can be done to alleviate and even to prevent the health and education casualties of youth.

Adolescence is a period of great risks and opportunities. The configuration of individual and social changes is unique in the life span. Adolescence can be a pathway to a productive adult life or to a vastly diminished existence. Its onset is a crucially formative phase of development. Puberty is a profound biological upheaval, and it coincides approximately with drastic changes in the social environment, especially the transition from elementary to junior high school or middle school. So it is a stressful time.

These early adolescent years, ten to fifteen, are open to the formation of behavior patterns in education and health that have lifelong significance. The dangerous patterns are only now beginning to get the public attention they deserve: becoming alienated from school and dropping out; starting to smoke cigarettes, drink alcohol, and use other drugs; starting to drive automobiles and motorcycles in high-risk ways; not eating a balanced diet or exercising enough; risking pregnancy and sexually transmitted diseases.

Initially, adolescents explore these new behaviors and possibilities tentatively. Before damaging patterns are firmly established, therefore, we have a major opportunity for intervention to prevent later casualties. Indeed, the formation of healthy lifestyles in this period can have a positive effect for the remainder of the life course. It is essential to help young adolescents acquire enduring self-esteem, inquiring habits of mind, reliable human relationships, a sense of belonging in a valued group, and a feeling of usefulness. Adolescents seek constructive expressions of their inherent curiosity and exploratory energy. They need a basis for making informed, deliberate decisions, especially on matters that have large consequences, such as educational and occupational futures, drug use, and human relationships.

Carnegie Corporation of New York established the Carnegie Council on Adolescent Development in 1986 to place the challenges of the adolescent years higher on the national agenda. Ruby Takanishi is the executive director and I serve as chairman. The Council stimulates interest in the risks and opportunities of the adolescent years and generates understanding of ways to facilitate the critical transition into adulthood.

Several major initiatives of the Council bear directly on facilitating healthy adolescent development. One is an effort to consolidate our science-based knowledge, which resulted in *At the Threshold: The Developing Adolescent*, edited by S. Shirley Feldman and Glen R. Elliott (Harvard University Press, 1990). The book has served to stimulate federal support of research on adolescent development and health.

Another is a collaborative effort between the U.S. Congress Office of Technology Assessment (OTA) and the Council, which produced the report series *Adolescent Health*. Vol. 1, *Summary and Policy Options;* vol. 2, *Background and the Effectiveness of Selected Prevention and Treatment Services*; and vol. 3, *Cross-*

cutting Issues in the Delivery of Health and Related Services (U.S. Government Printing Office, 1991). These reports probably constitute the most comprehensive review and analysis ever undertaken on this subject, incorporating specific policy options. Proposals are emerging in Congress to tackle the problems delineated in these reports.

Another activity resulted in *Turning Points: Preparing American Youth for the 21st Century* (Carnegie Council on Adolescent Development, 1989), a fundamental reassessment and drastic reformulation of education in the middle grade schools. The report was prepared by an interdisciplinary task force under the leadership of David W. Hornbeck and Anthony W. Jackson. It emphasized the intimate linkage of education and health in the schools—and the benefit to both of articulation with families and community organizations. Its recommendations elucidate important ways in which the pivotal institution of the middle grade school can improve prospects for healthy adolescent development. These recommendations have been implemented in a variety of state initiatives attuned to the developmental characteristics of adolescents.

A report on social support interventions was prepared by a working group of the Carnegie Council under the chairmanship of Richard H. Price. It clarifies the potential of schools, families, and community organizations to meet adolescent needs for social support by analyzing the research evidence on social support and carefully reviewing many support programs designed to respond to the needs of young adolescents. Similarly, the Council has published a report on life skills training, prepared by a working group under the chairmanship of Beatrix A. Hamburg. It synthesizes an extensive body of research showing how young adolescents can be taught life skills of great practical significance, especially skills requisite to effective decision making and coping as well as skills crucial for constructive human relationships.

The Council also initiated a multiauthor volume integrating a variety of disciplinary research literatures to compile a state-of-the-art assessment of adolescent health promotion that will be published in 1992 by Oxford University Press. This volume is edited by Susan G. Millstein, Anne C. Petersen, and Elena O. Nightingale.

The Council has created a task force under the leadership of James P. Comer, Wilma S. Tisch, and Jane Quinn to study neighborhood and community organizations that are or could be supportive of adolescents: youth agencies, religious youth groups, senior citizen groups, libraries, museums, recreation and sports programs, and after-school programs. The aim is to examine their current contributions and their potential for facilitating the development of young adolescents, particularly those in poverty.

Fred Hechinger has been an exceedingly valuable member of the Carnegie Council on Adolescent Development. He has for decades been one of America's most perceptive observers of children and youth. His distinguished writings for the *New York Times* have brilliantly illuminated issues of education and healthy child development. The cumulative record of his rich experience and knowledge, thoughtfully assessed at many points along the way, has produced authentic wisdom. So it was natural that the Council should turn to him to pull together its many health-related activities in a clear and cogent way for the general public.

One recurrent theme of the Council's studies is the inextricable linkage of health and education in the development of adolescents. This theme comes through vividly in the present report. The book integrates information and ideas from many sources, chiefly those stimulated by the Council but also other closely related studies. The recommendations are not those of the Council but rather of Fred Hechinger, arrived at after his careful consideration of the many recent studies in this field. The result is an intelligible, credible synthesis of knowledge and suggestions useful to the well-being of young people everywhere. They and we face fateful choices in creating healthy and productive lives for our common future.

DAVID A. HAMBURG
NEW YORK, JANUARY 1992

FATEFUL CHOICES

HEALTHY YOUTH FOR THE 21ST CENTURY

CHAPTER ONE

AT RISK

ADOLESCENTS IN

AMERICA TODAY

dolescence, in the popular view, is just an unfortunate "phase," something like a temporary illness from which, with time and perseverance, the "patient" will eventually recover. It is the butt of endless jokes, such as the observation widely attributed to Will Rogers that when he was fifteen years old he could not understand how his father could be so ignorant—then, by the time he was twenty-one, he was amazed at how much his dad had learned.

In reality, adolescence is no joke. While many adolescents do emerge from those turbulent years in good health, physically, intellectually, and emotionally, too many others are permanently damaged and many die—victims of an adult assumption that little can be done to alter their deleterious course.

In the 1990s, the state of adolescent health in America reached crisis proportions: large numbers of ten- to fifteen-year-olds suffer from depression that may lead to suicide; they jeopardize their future by abusing illegal drugs and alcohol, and by smoking; they engage in premature, unprotected sexual activity; they are victims or perpetrators of violence; they lack proper nutrition and exercise. Their glaring need for health services is largely ignored.

By age fifteen, about a quarter of all young adolescents are engaged in behaviors that are harmful or dangerous to themselves and others. Of 28 million adolescents between the ages of ten and eighteen, approximately 7 million are at serious risk of being harmed by health- and even life-threatening activity, as well as by school failure. Another 7 million are at moderate risk. Only half of the youngsters in this age group, or about 14 million, appear to be growing up basically healthy. But even these young people are not immune to risk since most of them at the very least lack sufficient problem-solving skills.

The years of early adolescence, roughly from the ages of ten to fifteen, mark the end of childhood and open up new vistas of the future—of options and goals—inviting speculation about adulthood in a world that holds all the possibilities of personal triumph and encourages dreams of glory. Early adolescence can be wondrous years.

They can also be frightening years. Those hopeful vistas of an unknown future can be dimmed by painful realities, by warnings of approaching storms, of the closing of options and of potential disasters. Adolescence can be a time of self-doubt, of loneliness, of fear of failure, of ambivalent relationships with peers and adults. These feelings can even raise the awesome question of whether or not life is worth living.

All adolescents are at a crossroads: these crucial years offer an opportunity to transform a period of high risk into one of high hopes. Given a chance, these young people can develop lives of great satisfaction to themselves and become the pride of their elders, their communities, and even their nation. But under present conditions, millions of them are not given that chance. They must be helped before it is too late.

Fateful choices confront young adolescents. If they are to choose wisely and thrive, they need understanding and help. Too many of them are raised in poverty and neglect, in homes that cannot provide physical safety, mental stimulation, or even minimal supervision. Some are without homes altogether.

The fateful choices are ours as a society as well, for, given sufficient attention and support, young people can have the chance to grow up healthy and whole both in body and in mind. What is at stake are not only the precious individual lives of our young people but our national health and our future as a nation.

THE TIME OF INTENSE CHANGE

Only the years from birth to age three, when the infant learns to walk, to speak, and to respond and acquires a host of skills, match adolescence in the intensity and rapidity of growth and change. Puberty unleashes new energies and desires. Adolescence itself has changed, and changed significantly, since the time when today's adults were teenagers. Whatever the reasons—which include better nutrition and the conquest of major infectious diseases—adolescence starts earlier. The onset of menstruation, for example, tends to occur at age twelve and a half, more than three years earlier than it did 150 years ago. This means that adolescents, barely past childhood, have adult powers of reproduction before they have developed the necessary reasoning powers that should be the guiding forces to procreation and parenthood. Yet, the biological drives and individual behavior cannot simply be put on hold until intellectual and ethical maturity catches up with sexual capacity.

Arriving at the threshold of adulthood, today's adolescents face the vast unknown with information that is constantly increasing but that is inadequate to prepare them for what lies ahead. Their minds and bodies are engaged in fierce battles between reason and emotion, between rebellion and accommodation. They must cope with those adults who regard as immature and foolish their many views, opinions, and goals that in the adolescent mind are sometimes agonizingly serious. Adolescents long for understanding and guidance. Too often their pleas are ignored, and their frustrated "acting out" is met with condemnation, punishment, or ridicule.

Adults need to learn to listen to youngsters, to begin the process of trying to understand them. In a study of inner-city adolescents, Professor Milbrey W. McLaughlin of Stanford University states: "Adolescents are not a lost cause. . . . Many people working in policy and funding areas seem to believe—incorrectly—that it's too late to intervene in the lives of anyone over the age of six."

A toddler climbs to the top of a bookcase. He is thrilled by his new accomplishment, this challenge to the world around him. Only recently has he learned to crawl, then walk. Now he has conquered new heights. But after he reaches the top, he is paralyzed with fear. There seems no way down. He has put himself at risk.

Fortunately, an adult—mother, father, or other care giver—comes to the rescue and guides a safe descent. No punishment awaits, no angry recrimination, only a quiet but firm explanation of why a climb into the unknown, without understanding the consequences, is dangerous and must not be repeated.

A climb into the unknown of a different nature may well be repeated some ten years later. Once again, the excitement of dangerous new powers, of new heights to climb, and new sensations to test may outpace the capacity to reason, to calculate the risks, or to judge the ability to climb down from a threatening height. Once again, the developing young person, now an adolescent, is at risk.

This time, the danger may be more serious, the rescue much more difficult. Yet, the rescue must be given the highest priority. If we make the mistake of believing that it is "too late" to intervene in the lives of our adolescents, the consequences might well be too great for us to measure.

For millions of young boys and girls, the ages between ten and fifteen are a time of hope and promise. But many unfortunate children are at great risk from the moment of birth, or even before; still others become particularly vulnerable during the early teenage years when economic deprivation and the normal developmental changes of adolescence coincide with the requirements of new intellectual tasks and the often inhospitable structure of junior high or middle school.

For too many youngsters, the future looks bleak: their prospects seem to be those of unemployment, poverty, and disintegrating families and communities. A significant number drop out of school, engage in violence or other criminal acts, be-

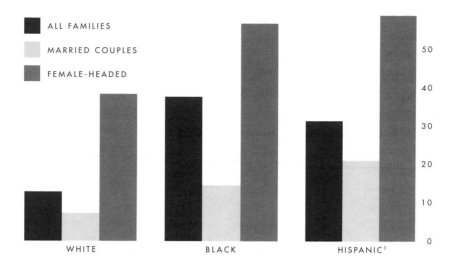

ALL FAMILIES

MARRIED COUPLES

FEMALE-HEADED

50

40

30

20

10

0

WHITE   BLACK   HISPANIC[1]

Families with Children Under 18 Years of Age Living Below the Poverty Level,[2] 1990

PERCENTAGE OF FAMILIES

Source: U.S. Bureau of the Census, Current Population Reports, Series P-60, no. 175, *Poverty in the United States: 1990* (Washington, D.C.: U.S. Government Printing Office, 1991).

[1] Hispanic people may be of any race.

[2] The poverty level is set in direct proportion to the Consumer Price Index and varies by family size. In 1990, the poverty level for a family of four was an annual household income below $13,359.

come pregnant, suffer mental disorders, abuse drugs and/or alcohol, attempt suicide, are disabled by injuries, or die.

All too many adolescents find their own neighborhoods so dangerous that they fear walking to school; some even arm themselves with weapons. Searching for security and peer approval, they become sexually active earlier than did their parents.

In addition to the developmental changes they undergo, today's young adolescents are bombarded by messages on television, in the movies, and in magazines that glorify casual, unprotected sexual intercourse as glamorous, portray alcohol and cigarettes as symbols of maturity, and hold out the accumulation

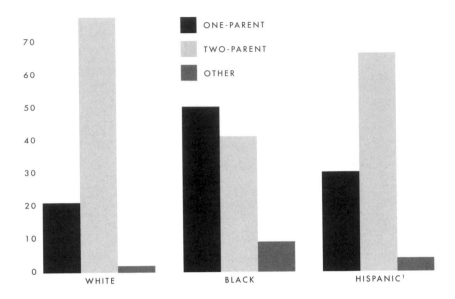

Living Arrangements of Adolescents 10 to 17 Years Old, 1990

PERCENTAGE OF ADOLESCENTS

Source: U.S. Bureau of the Census, Current Population Reports, Series P-20, no. 450, *Marital Status and Living Arrangements: March 1990* (Washington, D.C.: U.S. Government Printing Office, 1991).

[1] Hispanic people may be of any race.

of consumer goods as the measure of success and status. The implication is that self-indulgence is a virtue and that crime pays.

The sad reality is that young adolescents at every economic level are very often neglected by adults—even within their own families—or get lost in the mass, victims of large institutions that undermine their healthy development. Many young people attend schools that ignore their needs and capabilities. They return from school to empty homes and suffer the consequences of anonymity—a scourge of modern society and a condition that makes people, young and old, behave at their worst. "Every child," says Joy G. Dryfoos in *Adolescents at Risk*, "needs to be attached to a responsible adult who pays attention to that child's individual needs."

Being young and facing the future is difficult in a world of great economic uncertainties. For those young people who fail to complete high school, there are few jobs. If they have the added liability of living in inner cities amid poverty and pervasive unemployment, it is particularly hard for them to look ahead with any confidence. Most of the role models around them are negative: men without work and overburdened women without husbands struggling against tremendous odds to feed and shelter their families. They face the ever-present threat of violence and the emotional and economic lures of using and selling drugs.

The social consequences of these realities have never been so tangible. America's demographic composition has undergone dramatic changes. Nearly 40 percent of youths entering the work force now come from black, Latino, and Asian families; to become successful, they must have skills that allow them to move into the mainstream. More than ever before, national and community leadership must be held responsible for helping this generation of teenagers enter a society that offers genuine equality and opportunity for all people, including minorities and women. Unless today's adolescents are convinced that there is hope for them in the future, they will drop out—not only from school but from society as well.

Many young people believe, because of the conditions surrounding them, that equality of opportunity does not exist; so they give up. This creates a vicious circle: talents are squandered, teenagers are ill prepared, employment is denied, at-risk behavior is reinforced. Adrift in a desolate and often hostile environment, these young people desperately need adults to whom they can turn with trust for guidance and support.

Elena O. Nightingale, special adviser to Carnegie Corporation's president, says: "The relative isolation of adolescents from adults contributes to the view of adolescence as an alien subculture with no meaningful role in society." Lacking a more clearly defined role, teenagers often feel useless.

Teenagers are full of curiosity, energy, imagination, and,

given encouragement, idealism. Adults must take care not to ridicule or diminish young people's convictions that the world is capable of being improved. Sometimes adolescents issue challenges or even provoke arguments as a means of testing adult views or merely to get a credible response. The questions they ask deserve answers. What kind of person am I? Does anybody care? Can I make a difference? How can school help me in my future? How can I become more popular? What can I do to become better looking? Get stronger? Am I making a fool of myself? Why are some people poor? Can't the system be fixed to work better, to be more fair?

Foolish questions? Not if adults understand what is at stake for those who ask them. They are questions generated by the search for identity and self-esteem. Not to take them seriously is to block the adolescent's road to maturity. Again and again, studies show that adolescents lack an adequate basis for making conscious decisions, because they have not been given adequate answers to such crucial questions as How can I use my own body wisely? What lies ahead for me in adult life?

In a draft of a forthcoming book, *Adolescent Health Promotion*, Lisa J. Crockett and Anne C. Petersen of Pennsylvania State University stress: "To support a healthy sense of self-esteem, adolescents need opportunities to feel competent and successful. . . . One strategy is to help them discover their talents and develop their feelings of competence in valued domains. This means improving young people's competence in traditionally approved areas such as academics, but it may also mean supporting areas of competence outside scholastic achievement to enable less academically gifted students to develop a sense of pride in their accomplishments."

Sharon Kravitz, a teacher in Public School 85 in the Bronx, asked pupils to write an opera based on their own experiences in their homes and neighborhoods. The project was a success. Some fifth- and sixth-graders who had barely responded to questions a year earlier suddenly bubbled over with enthusiasm. "Give them a sense of accomplishment," Ms. Kravitz told the *New York Times.* "They can blossom."

Today, the failure of adolescents to grow into physically, mentally, and spiritually healthy adults will ultimately turn a substantial number of them into men and women who are without humane values and without a sense of what is right or wrong. This dangerous and debilitating lack of values is as much a threat to affluent youth, who can become candidates for white-collar crimes of greed, corruption, and exploitation, as it is for poor young people, who may drift into other forms of criminal behavior, violence, and corruption. Rich or poor, young people are in danger of turning to illicit drugs and to alcohol in an attempt to escape from the self-doubt and anxiety that haunts them when their future seems so uncertain, and perhaps even threatening.

The challenge in responding to these threats and to the needs of young adolescents is to remove the barriers that block the way to successful development and constructive behavior. It is the responsibility of adults to address the problems facing youths, for whom this stage of life represents the last best chance to enter adulthood whole in mind, body, and spirit.

Responsible attention to young adolescents must begin with an understanding that this age group is not homogeneous. It consists of many subgroups, which, though they face common problems, must also deal with a variety of different experiences related to their social, ethnic, or racial backgrounds. For example, black male adolescents are five to six times as likely to die as a result of homicide as white males, and black girls are two to three times as likely to become homicide victims as white girls. Thus, the degree of teenagers' specific risks depends in large measure on their ethnicity and on how society responds to it. In California and Texas, more than half of the children in the public schools are Hispanic or of nonwhite background. In many urban centers, such as New York City, more than 70 percent of the public school enrollment is nonwhite. According to Census Bureau forecasts, by the end of the century, 20 percent of the country's youths are expected to be black and 18 percent Hispanic.

American families are under great stress. One in four American youths grows up with only one parent, usually the mother. More than half of black adolescents are in households without a father. More than 60 percent of mothers with adolescent children are in the labor force. A study by psychologists at the University of Chicago found that teenagers in two-parent homes spend less than forty minutes a day with their mothers and less than five minutes a day alone with their fathers.

This is a far cry indeed from the idealized traditional family in which the mother cared for the children, the home, and the kitchen while the father was the breadwinner, and the children were safe in a benevolent school from which they returned home to do their homework, secure in the hearth of family life.

Contemporary youngsters are lucky if they do not suffer, in addition to the strains of a single-parent family, the pain of poverty. At present, one in five young adolescents aged ten to fifteen lives in poverty. In absolute numbers, most poor children are white, but a higher proportion of black and Hispanic children are living in poverty: 45 and 41 percent, respectively, compared to 13 percent for white youths. Families headed by women are more likely than other families to live in poverty: 46 percent of female-headed households are impoverished. While the median income for all American families is above $30,000, those headed by women with children have a median income of only about $9,000.

Adding to the social and economic instability of the contemporary family is a population on the move: between 1985 and 1990, 40 percent of ten- to fourteen-year-olds moved to new homes; almost half of them moved to different counties, thus experiencing the emotional turmoil of adjusting to unfamiliar people, schools, and communities.

In recent years, poverty has also reduced many families to homelessness. An estimated 2.5 million children are now living in domiciles other than homes. Many of them do not attend school regularly, and often they grow up amidst drug and alcohol abuse, crime, and violence.

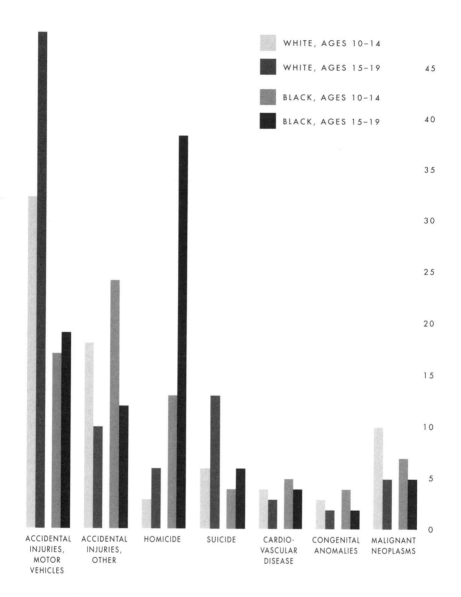

☐	WHITE, AGES 10–14
■	WHITE, AGES 15–19
■	BLACK, AGES 10–14
■	BLACK, AGES 15–19

Estimated Mortality from Seven Leading Causes for White and Black Adolescents 10 to 14 and 15 to 19 Years Old, 1987

PERCENTAGE OF DEATHS

Source: U.S. Congress Office of Technology Assessment, *Adolescent Health.* Vol. 1, *Summary and Policy Options*, OTA-H-468 (Washington, D.C.: U.S. Government Printing Office, April 1991).

THE RISKS

The conditions described above have put many young adolescents at risk. They endanger their health and often their lives. While many of these dangers are products of the environment, they are often also the consequence of typically adolescent behavior. Adolescents, for example, put themselves at risk by not using safety belts while in cars, by not wearing helmets while riding bicycles, by the careless handling of firearms, and by engaging in unprotected sex. The principal causes of adolescent illness and death are accidents, homicide, suicide, substance abuse, and the consequences of reckless sexual activity. Added to the list of risky behaviors to which adolescents are prone is reckless driving. Adolescent drivers have a higher rate of passenger and driver fatalities than adults. In recent years, skateboarding has also been added to the list of common injuries.

In 1986, of 3,264 deaths in the twelve to fourteen age group, 7 percent died of suicide and 6 percent of homicide. Of the 8,203 deaths among fifteen- to seventeen-year-olds, suicide accounted for 11 percent of the deaths and homicide for 9 percent. A 1990 survey of 1,152 young people between the ages of thirteen and nineteen commissioned by Empire Blue Cross and Blue Shield and conducted by the Gallup organization showed that 6 percent attempted suicide; 15 percent said they came "very close to trying." Three out of five youngsters said they knew a teenager who had actually committed suicide. Nearly half of those in the survey cited family or other home problems as the major reason for contemplating or attempting suicide. Other causes listed were depression, problems with friends and the opposite sex, and feelings of worthlessness. Most of the young people said that they thought some progress in helping teenagers had been made, but 80 percent still believed that communities, schools, and religious institutions should do more to help them cope with their problems.

While the actual number of adolescent suicides may appear

low, it seems certain that there is a much higher number of un-reported attempted suicide; an even larger number contemplate suicide, attributable to untreated mental health problems and other conditions that put young people at risk.

Even when allowances are made for teenagers' tendency to dramatize their emotions, it is clear that many young ado-lescents find it difficult to cope with the stress they face in their daily lives. Adults who ignore this reality do so at young people's peril. To treat adolescent problems lightly, or to en-gage in wishful thinking without taking the necessary mea-sures to remove the many obstacles to healthy adolescent de-velopment, is to court disaster. Such neglect truly places a generation at risk.

Despite the frequency with which adolescents report suici-dal feelings, they themselves do not place suicide at the top of the list of their concerns. They report that the issues that trou-ble them most are their grades in school, uncertainties about their future jobs and careers, and, more generally, "problems of growing up."

The extent of depression among adolescents is not easy to document. A white paper issued by the American Medical As-sociation in 1990 indicated that 16 percent of male youth and 19 percent of females between the ages of thirteen and eighteen suffer from depression; there is mounting evidence that de-pression often leads to drugs and alcohol.

Susan G. Millstein points out, in a paper prepared for the Carnegie Council on Adolescent Development, that the way adolescents perceive—and report—their health status can be quite contradictory: they often minimize their symptoms or deny them entirely; on the other hand, they may also exagger-ate them. While they acknowledge a wide variety of health is-sues, they tend to rank only a relatively few as of major concern, among them school-related problems, attention to their teeth and vision, mental health, acne, and relationships with others. By contrast, substance use, sexual behavior, nutrition, and ex-ercise tend to be ranked lower.

As adolescents grow older, their mental health becomes more important to them. Like adults, they generally define their condition in terms of how they feel—whether or not they are content and happy or sad and depressed. The majority of adolescents report being satisfied with their lives, but studies in San Francisco and Minnesota have shown that about 25 percent feel dissatisfied—a minority, but still a sizable number. Girls, Millstein found, reported a greater sense of satisfaction than boys.

It would be naive to ignore adolescents' worries about their future as unrelated to their mental health. Increasing numbers of adolescents grow up in poverty. Currently, half of black, Hispanic, and American Indian and almost one-third of Asian-American adolescents are poor or "near" poor. And most are keenly aware of the severe limitations that restrict their access to future economic success. A survey of more than 500 adolescents by the American Home Economics Association found that financial issues were of major concern, especially among black and Hispanic youths, who worried not only about paying for an education but also about the country's economy. Sixty percent of all the adolescents in the sample believed that their lives will be more difficult than their parents', and 34 percent worried about making wrong decisions about their future and their ability to change their decisions later on.

Not all was gloom. Many youngsters were optimistic about going to college and hoped that they would find jobs they could enjoy. In a sample taken in Minnesota, 60 percent saw themselves as energetic and believed that life was full of interesting opportunities.

Yet, whether they report feeling optimistic or pessimistic, adolescents clearly are concerned about the next steps in their lives. They worry. And for a substantial number, their mental well-being hangs in the balance.

ACKNOWLEDGING THE RISKS

Reducing the risks to adolescents' well-being obviously calls for the regular use of health services. Yet, adolescents as a group tend either to ignore their needs for these services or to have limited access to them.

About 12 percent of American adolescents have no regular provider of medical care. Even though 12,784 middle or junior high schools now exist in the United States, only a few are served by health centers. (For details, see chapter 2.) In addition, the cooperation between schools and community social service agencies is often poor or nonexistent.

Almost all of the centers are inadequately funded, especially in poor communities where the need is greatest. But there is little doubt about the effectiveness of the few health centers that are now linked to the schools. Where they exist, they are used. For example, while almost half of those adolescents who are treated in more traditional settings away from their schools miss their scheduled return appointments, only 5.6 percent of those using school-related centers were reported to do so. Equally impressive are relative costs—$11.25 for a routine physical check-up at a school-related center, compared to $45 in a private physician's office. Counting the lost wages of a parent accompanying an adolescent raises the cost to more than $59.

Apart from issues of cost, it is a fact widely ignored, including by many parents, that many adolescents experience acute health problems; despite this, they seek medical care less often than do other age groups. The underutilization of health services is greatest among young adolescents, members of minority groups, and, as might be expected, the poor. Among the chief obstacles, according to Susan G. Millstein and Iris F. Litt, writing in *At the Threshold*, are the poor organization and the limited availability of health services, as well as the lack of confidentiality.

Moreover, few health service providers are trained in managing this age group. The authors continue: "Providers may convey to adolescent patients their discomfort in discussing topics such as sexuality, which may result in adolescents' unwillingness to raise sensitive issues that concern them. Because young people are frequently considered difficult to work with, practitioners may not want to devote the time needed to establish strong rapport with them."

Another obstacle is that adolescents resist treatments that may unfavorably affect their appearance. Because the refusal to follow professional recommendations can have serious consequences, it is particularly important that, in administering to adolescents, the health provider be able to build strong personal trust. The young person must feel that the recommendation is coming from someone who understands his or her emotions and fears and who truly cares about the patient on a personal, not simply a professional, level. Because professional health providers often appear distant and impersonal, it is easy for young adolescents to shy away from them and ignore their recommendations. Physicians, nurses, and other health providers who treat this age group need special training in understanding the feelings and emotions of young adolescents if they are to maintain their confidence.

By the same token, adults should not assume that a young person, simply because he or she knows what is harmful, will act accordingly. Like many of their elders, adolescents often engage in wishful thinking and the hope that health problems will simply disappear, that they will personally escape the consequences of what they know to be harmful behavior, and that this behavior will be easily corrected as they "grow up." This is rarely so, of course, and in the case of behavior that threatens to turn into addiction, it is a dangerous self-delusion. It is as perilous for young people to place irrational faith in the corrective power of future adulthood as it is for parents and other adults to shrug helplessly in the face of undesirable or dangerous adolescent behavior, in the expectation that the difficult "phase" will pass on its own accord.

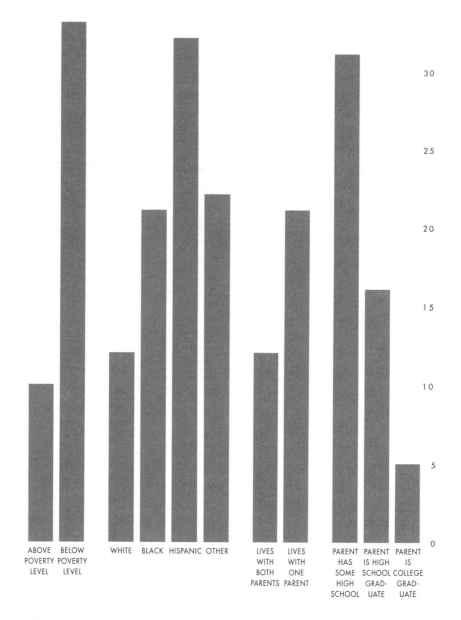

30

25

20

15

10

5

0

| ABOVE POVERTY LEVEL | BELOW POVERTY LEVEL | | WHITE | BLACK | HISPANIC | OTHER | | LIVES WITH BOTH PARENTS | LIVES WITH ONE PARENT | | PARENT HAS SOME HIGH SCHOOL | PARENT IS HIGH SCHOOL GRAD-UATE | PARENT IS COLLEGE GRAD-UATE |

Characteristics of Adolescents 10 to 18 Years Old Without Health Insurance

PERCENTAGE OF ADOLESCENTS

Source: P. W. Newacheck and M. A. McManus (1991). Original tabulations from the 1986 National Health Interview Survey.

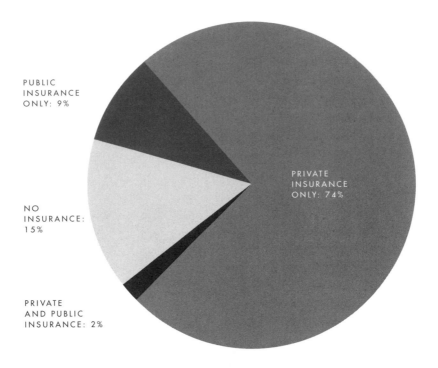

PUBLIC
INSURANCE
ONLY: 9%

PRIVATE
INSURANCE
ONLY: 74%

NO
INSURANCE:
15%

PRIVATE
AND PUBLIC
INSURANCE: 2%

Health Insurance Coverage of Adolescents 10 to 18 Years Old

PERCENTAGE OF COVERAGE

Source: P. W. Newacheck and M. A. McManus (1991). Original tabulations from the 1986 National Health Interview Survey.

I n 1990, a report called *Code Blue: Uniting for a Healthier Youth*, by the National Association of State Boards of Education and the American Medical Association, warned that never before has one generation of American adolescents been less healthy, less cared for, or less prepared for life than their parents were at the same age. *Code Blue* raised an alarm that the state of adolescent health in America today constitutes a national emergency. The commission preparing the report conceded that many adolescents are doing well against all odds and that there are families, schools, communities, and government programs that offer encouraging success stories. But as the commission pointed out, such positive stories merely drive home the fact that serious harm can be prevented if the emergency is properly addressed.

Our current health-care system, where it functions well at all, tends to respond to specific complaints rather than concentrating on the prevention of trouble. The system is fragmented into many different specialties and subspecialties. It leaves it to young people to negotiate when and how their health should get attention. Lacking proper guidance, they seldom make any effort to do so.

Cost is a key factor. Among young people between the ages of ten and eighteen, about 14 percent have no health insurance. The percentage is far worse among minorities and the poor. Altogether, 9 to 12 million children have no health insurance, and millions of others have inadequate coverage. Many find even low-cost clinics beyond their means. One out of three poor adolescents is not covered by Medicaid, and adolescents in the southern states are the most likely to be uninsured. In a poor national economy, some families are forced to reduce or eliminate insurance for their dependent children, and employers often cut or discontinue such benefits as a condition for not laying off workers. Most private insurance plans do not cover services that are particularly important for adolescent well-being, such as basic dental, hearing, vision, and maternity-related benefits. Mental health and substance abuse treatment costs are often limited or altogether excluded under these policies. Unless they belong to health maintenance organizations, adolescents usually are not covered at all for preventive health services.

Effective care—acute as well as preventive—calls for comprehensive facilities. *Code Blue* described the following example of a good comprehensive health care program for teens:

Jackson, Mississippi, is the center for eight urban and rural school-based health centers that serve children from preschool through high school. The first center was established in 1979 out of the concern of two local physicians who were giving free physicals to young athletes. The physicians became very worried about the kind of health problems they were finding among the students—urinary tract infections, heart murmurs, hypertension, and more. It made them wonder about the health of other students, especially those who could not afford regular health checkups.

Available services at the centers include routine and acute medical and dental care, counseling, health education, pregnancy prevention, and services for teen mothers. Students must have parental consent to participate. Among the centers' accomplishments: 7,273 adolescents and preadolescents have been served—an almost equal mix of males and females. None of the 182 participating teen mothers have dropped out of school, although about 50 percent of pregnant teens had dropped out prior to the program's existence.

Program staff credit their success to strong support from the school, families, and the community—in fact, they feel that these are essential ingredients for success.

Code Blue also urged the creation of local coordinating councils as alliances of elected officials, agency heads, school and public health officials, private service providers, civic, business, and religious leaders, families, and youths. It stressed the importance of "organizing services around people, not people around services."

Poverty in itself poses special risks to young people's health, quite apart from their inability to pay for adequate health care. The very fact that, despite their serious disadvantages, many adolescents who grow up poor manage to beat the odds and mature to healthy adulthood is testimony to an amazing reservoir of strength. This underscores what massive benefits could be reaped if more adequate health care were to be provided for children of poverty.

In addition to the consequences of poverty and lack of insurance, proper health care for adolescents is undermined by a serious shortage of trained personnel, inadequate information about services that may be available, and the inability of many working adults to accompany their young adolescents to health providers. Almost entirely overlooked are the several hundred

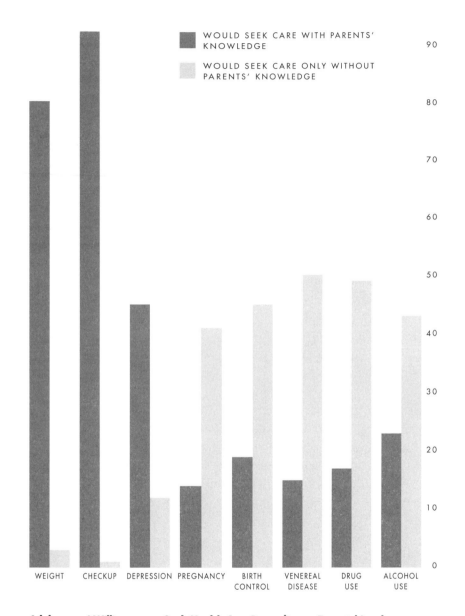

Adolescents' Willingness to Seek Health Care Depending on Parental Involvement

PERCENTAGE OF ADOLESCENTS

Source: A. Marks, J. Malizio, J. Hoch, R. Brody, and M. Fisher (1983). "Assessment of Health Needs and Willingness to Utilize Health Care Resources of Adolescents in a Suburban Population," *Journal of Pediatrics* 102: 456–60.

thousand adolescents living in juvenile justice facilities, thus adding to their already dismal situation the prospect of troubled health as their legacy.

This book views adolescent health in its broadest sense. For example, it recognizes that school failure is a key indicator of an adolescent's vulnerability to a broad range of dangers. School failure is often itself a symptom of much else that is troubling in an adolescent's life, such as poor nutrition, lack of sleep, chronic and untreated illness, a disorganized home, or a threatening environment. Poor health in all its dimensions, including the problem of depression, clearly interferes with performance in school. It could, therefore, be misleading to rely on reports of school failure as the diagnosis of an adolescent's vulnerability. Instead, school failure may be a warning that a teenager's health needs attention, or that an unhealthy environment rather than limited talent is the cause of poor academic performance.

In any assessment of adolescent health, and of attitudes and behavior that place young people at risk, it would be seriously misleading to regard only inner-city minority teenagers or those living in rural poverty as vulnerable. As already noted, adolescents across the social and economic spectrums are at serious risk, even though the nature of the risks may differ. All need attention, even while the conditions under which poor youngsters grow up call for special priorities in social reform and improved access to health care.

Just as growing up affluent is no protection against the risks of ill health or failure, growing up poor does not eliminate the possibility of success and a future of well-being. From Harlem's Adam Clayton Powell Junior High School, the Raging Rooks have made a name for themselves, not only in their neighborhood but in tournaments played across the country. These black teenagers are not part of a basketball team or a rock group. "Rook" is not a typographical error: it refers to a chess team, and these teenagers are champions. In 1991, they tied for first place in the National Junior High Chess Championship sponsored by the United States Chess Federation.

As reported in the *New York Times*, when they encounter the stares of onlookers in airports or hotel lobbies and they tell their questioners that they are a chess team, says Kasaun Henry, the fourteen-year-old captain, "people look baffled and say, 'What?' It's stupid, but we try not to let it upset us. We just concentrate on our chess."

That their teenage children will overcome the lures of activities less beneficial than chess can hardly be taken for granted by parents at any economic level today. The mother of one of the Rooks talked about the neighborhood around the school and the four crack houses around the corner from her home. "There's everything on the streets, but these kids walk right by it," she said. "All they do is play chess once the homework is done. It's such a pleasure when they are playing at our house. It's quiet and you hear the pieces clicking, and it's like being in another world. You can really feel your child will never get involved with all that out there."

The chess team did not simply appear out of nowhere. The club was started twenty years ago by Richard Gudonsky, a science teacher who is a moderately good chess player. Six years ago, he started taking the boys to tournaments. Then, with the help of the Manhattan Chess Club School, he managed to secure the services of Maurice Ashley, a black chess professional who, he said, is a superb coach. "He is just the kind of man these boys need in their lives."

And that is the point. Any activity that tests and evokes youngsters' talents and builds belief in themselves could do as much. The adults who built their self-confidence—the man the boys needed in their lives and the mother who nurtured their success—are the keys. So were the celebratory banners that greeted them in their school, and the delighted congratulations.

Access to success is not always easy, but the ingredients are much the same. As reported in the *New York Times* (June 9,

1991), Kevin Wilson, who in 1991 was graduated from Oliver High School in Pittsburgh sixth in a class of 182, is attending college. He ascribes his success to his father, a railroad worker who never finished high school and was stabbed to death in 1988. Kevin recalls his father telling him: "To get farther, to compete with all the white people and all, you've got to get an education." He remembers that his father sometimes would wake him during the night and ask him to repeat: "I am somebody."

For Charmaine Benson, eighteen, another of the school's graduates, the road to success was harder, but not very different from that traveled by countless numbers of poverty's children. Her mother left school at fourteen when she was pregnant and has rarely been employed; her father was killed on the streets when she was two; she grew up in a housing project often torn by violence. When Charmaine showed her mother her good grades, she sneered and accused Charmaine of "trying to be better than anybody else." But even in the face of her liabilities, Charmaine gets up daily at 5:00 A.M. and travels by bus across the city to attend a school far away from her depressing neighborhood. She is able to negotiate not only the physical distance from an unsupportive home but the emotional distance as well. Fortunately, one of her teachers helped her to prepare for college and also took her on her first trip out of the city. Charmaine wants to be a teacher.

A necdotes are not policy, but they are powerful in shaping policies. They can illustrate hidden strengths. They can dispel the hopelessness that leads to inaction. This book aims to shape policies that will nurture those neglected strengths and talents wherever they are, amid poverty or affluence.

While the recovery of adolescents from damage already incurred is an essential aspect of this book, it is even more crucial to focus on preventing health-threatening behavior and promoting the attitudes and habits that generate health. This calls for a society that is committed to promoting health among all its citizens. Singling out one age group is not enough; life, after all, is lived in continuity. Damaging attitudes about nutrition, alcohol, drugs, tobacco, and sexual practices cannot be transformed within any single age group; they respond to standards set by the whole of society.

What follows is a synthesis of current research findings about the experience of adolescents in America today and an attempt to identify the urgent measures that will be required so that, at age fifteen or soon thereafter, adolescents will emerge

▲ Sound of mind and body
▲ Firmly grounded in the basic skills and in critical thinking
▲ Responsible in using their new sexual powers and building stable personal and family ties
▲ Armed against the lures of addiction to alcohol, drugs, and cigarettes
▲ Intellectually and morally prepared for the world of work and the responsibilities and rewards of good citizenship in a free society

The ultimate goal of the book is to connect adolescents with their futures by presenting them with constructive links to adulthood through guidance by caring adults who know that to neglect them is to put all of our futures at risk.

CHAPTER TWO

PREVENTING DAMAGE

What happens to adolescents is in many ways a reflection of what happens to adults. The prevailing attitude about health focuses on the cure of illness rather than on its prevention, and the medical profession itself is still far more attuned to treating disease than it is to promoting good health.

However, for adolescents there is a crucial difference: preventive health care for that age group is especially important and rewarding because it can set the course for many years of healthy adult life. The patterns of thought and behavior established during these formative years can effectively break the cycle of risks that are not only dangerous to the adolescents but are overwhelmingly costly to society. If patterns of health-giving behavior follow a nurturing childhood, preceded by proper prenatal care to assure a healthy pregnancy, a vast range of problems can be prevented. Even for those deprived of a well-cared-for and constructive infancy, the adolescent years usually offer the last best chance to reduce the risks and enhance the opportunities for becoming healthy adults.

In its 1991 report on adolescent health, the U.S. Congress Office of Technology Assessment made a point of the many factors and sources that contribute to young people's well-being. "Put positively, adolescents who do well seem to have strong and developmentally appropriate social support, preferably

from their families, but if not from their families, from some other adult or adults. Similarly, schools that are small, comfortable, safe, and intellectually engaging and emotionally intimate communities, can also make a difference in adolescent health and well-being."

Young people must feel that health-care providers, particularly those who are engaged in the prevention of harm, are empathetic and easily accessible. Otherwise, the services will be offered in a vacuum, with few young people disposed to take advantage of them and a consequent high rate of health crises on the part of those who go uncounseled and untreated.

Experienced and well-trained health providers who treat the health problems of young people are scarce, especially when the adolescents in question are poor and uninsured. Donald Cohen, a psychiatrist at Yale University, explains: "Professionals go where the money is, where success is most likely, and where it's easy to provide their services. That's why the problem doesn't get defined in terms of family or social needs, but in terms of what works for the professionals."

Lisbeth B. Schorr modifies that judgment somewhat in *Within Our Reach*: "Many professionals would be willing and able to work more effectively with high-risk children if their training gave them the requisite skills and exposed them to relevant experiences, and if they worked in a setting which assigned higher rewards to doing so."

She also points to the failing of professionals who work with young adolescents to address young people's psychological problems. She asks: "Should child psychiatry and medicine not be striving constantly to respond to the social forces that affect the children who come to them for help?" To demonstrate the peril of not assuming such responsibility, she cites the example of a psychiatrist at a major children's hospital who noted in his evaluation after spending two hours with a twelve-year-old girl that she was sexually active, but he had not discussed contraception with her, nor had he referred her to family planning services.

Writing in the *Journal of Adolescent Health Care* (May

1990), Lawrence S. Friedman et al. say that primary-care physicians "are in a unique position to identify substance-abusing adolescents." Yet, they report that interviews with fifty-four substance-abusing adolescents and their parents showed that as many as 43 percent did not recall being asked by the examining physicians about whether they used alcohol and other drugs. The authors conclude that "some physicians may not identify adolescents as being at high risk for active substance abuse. Despite the fact that virtually all our subjects had an encounter with a physician during a time of abuse, less than half recalled being asked about alcohol or recreational drug use. A background of poor school performance or visits to the emergency room for drug-related problems did not appear to increase the probability that an adolescent would recall being asked about drug or alcohol use." The fault did not seem entirely with the physicians' response. The authors also found that most parents did not think of their doctor as a resource in dealing with their childrens' drug or alcohol use. In addition, many adolescents were found not to be replying honestly to questions about substance use, especially in the presence of their parents.

Medical schools and postgraduate medical education often place little emphasis on the diagnosis and treatment of these matters. Primary-care physicians appear reluctant to spend the time and energy necessary to deal with psychosocial issues. These call for a form of counseling that produces less financial reward than uncomplicated or procedure-oriented office visits.

The lack of knowledge among many physicians about substance abuse by young people points to more general deficiencies in the training and attitudes of many health-care providers—deficiencies that seriously hamper the professionals' ability to detect and prevent undesirable and dangerous adolescent behavior.

In the *Journal of Adolescent Health Care* (July 1990), Robert W. Blum and Linda H. Bearinger report on a national survey of 3,066 physicians, nurses, social workers, nutritionists, and psychologists concerning their knowledge and attitudes about adolescent health care. A substantial number of physicians and nurses reported that they lacked competence in the areas of eating disorders, learning disabilities, chronic illnesses, and delinquent behavior. More than half of the psychologists interviewed admitted lack of competence in discussing sexual issues, dealing with eating disorders, and treating chronic illness. And, nearly half of the nutritionists questioned reported that they lacked knowledge about adolescent food-related concerns.

Regrettably, there appeared to be no incentive to correct the situation. Although almost half of the physicians believed that their training was insufficient, only 27 percent showed interest in developing better skills when confronting teenagers' problems.

"Pediatricians are used to having patients who don't talk back, and adolescents talk back," Jennifer Johnson, an assistant professor at the University of Oklahoma Medical College, told *Education Week* (December 4, 1991).

Paul Jellinek, vice president of the Robert Wood Johnson Foundation, agrees: "Taking care of adolescents is a very tricky business, since it involves a lot of social and behavioral issues that are not part of most mainstream training programs."

Richard MacKenzie, associate professor of pediatrics at the University of Southern California's School of Medicine, told reporters at the 1991 convention of the American Academy of Pediatrics that he always tries to let an adolescent know that he or she is the focus of his professional attention.

As of 1991, the Society of Adolescent Medicine estimated that there are no more than 1,000 physicians who specialize in dealing with that age group nationwide. According to the Office of Technology Assessment, only about sixty young doctors are enrolled in adolescent medicine training programs in any given year. Starting in 1993, the medical profession will formally recognize adolescent medicine as a medical subspecialty.

Meanwhile, it is not surprising that social workers, finding little reward in the often disturbing business of working with disadvantaged youngsters and their families, are turning in

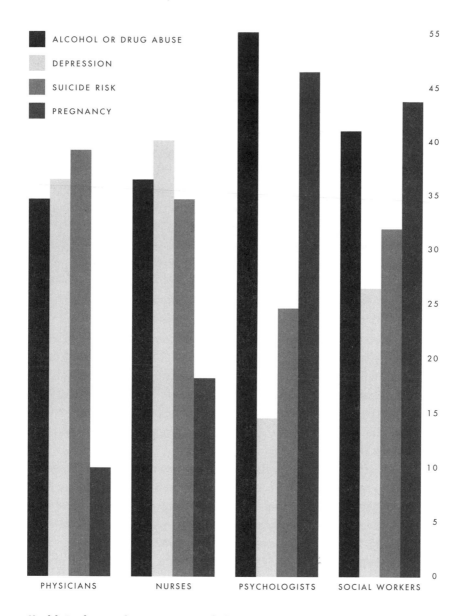

■	ALCOHOL OR DRUG ABUSE
	DEPRESSION
	SUICIDE RISK
	PREGNANCY

PHYSICIANS　　NURSES　　PSYCHOLOGISTS　　SOCIAL WORKERS

Health Professionals' Assessment of Their Training in Adolescent Health

PERCENTAGE FEELING INADEQUATELY TRAINED

Source: R. W. Blum and L. H. Bearinger (1990). "Knowledge and Attitudes of
Health Professionals Toward Adolescent Health Care," *Journal of Adolescent
Health Care* 11: 289–94.

great numbers to more lucrative private practice. Even more damaging to young people is the fact that, while teachers know that physical and psychological problems get in the way of many of their pupils' academic achievements, their training has not prepared them to address the nonacademic problems that youngsters inevitably bring with them to school.

What emerges is the necessity for a revival of John Dewey's concept of "the whole child"—the importance of paying equal and simultaneous attention to the physical, mental, and psychological development of young people. It is precisely when human beings are not looked at in their totality, and their care is assigned to a variety of separate systems, separate institutions, and different specialists, that serious problems go undetected and often are aggravated.

One characteristic of a fragmented system is that in an effort to minimize cost, preventive measures take the form of passive instruction, through films, videos, brochures, and posters. While there is some value in these tools, if they are not combined with personalized instruction, they are not likely to change adolescent attitudes and behavior. Indeed, the world in which today's adolescents live is so different from that experienced by previous generations that young people now require instruction and models about how to cope with life itself.

What are the life skills necessary for survival, and how are they to be acquired? Does the future hold promise as well as threat? How does one learn to live with other people? Even the most successful, capable parents cannot teach their children the wide array of skills needed in today's enormously complex and constantly changing society. When a home is further burdened by poverty and other dysfunctions such as those created by alcohol or drug abuse, parents are particularly ill equipped to even attempt to teach their children how to behave and thrive.

TEACHING LIFE SKILLS

One response to modern society's demands is the development of life skills training. Its purpose is to teach adolescents how to form relationships, how to use social systems, how to develop healthy behavior, and how to allow their intellectual curiosity a wide range.

In the past, these skills would normally be acquired from family, church, friends, and the school. As these influences have grown less compelling, young adolescents need adults who can be positive role models and mentors. They need sources of information from authorities they can trust, especially on matters that affect their development and long-term health. They need help in trying to perceive the changes taking place in their bodies. They need to learn communication skills and how to regulate their behavior. And they need instruction and support in learning how to solve problems and make decisions.

The speed with which life has changed is put into perspective by the fact that, at the turn of the century, only 10 percent of American adolescents attended school. Yet, while schools today play a key role, both academically and socially, in the lives of virtually all adolescents, the schools have barely begun to adjust to the new social responsibilities that have been foisted on them. For example, though teenagers are constantly under a barrage of messages delivered by television, radio, and pop music—usually in isolation from adults—schools have hardly begun to teach them how to view and listen critically. Yet, such a capacity for critical analysis ought to be a major component of life skills education.

To underscore the problem, the media, and particularly television, play a major role in modeling adolescent sexual behavior. According to *TV Guide*, American television viewers are annually exposed "to some 9,230 scenes of suggested sexual intercourse or innuendo," and "fully 94 percent of the sex on soap operas involves people not married to each other." Likewise, in the sexual intercourse portrayed in motion pictures, on videocassettes, and in rock music, nobody appears to be concerned with contraceptives. Nobody seems to worry about pregnancy.

In 1990, the Carnegie Council on Adolescent Development sponsored efforts to review a life skills training program that would teach adolescents vital skills for surviving, living with others, and succeeding in a complex and rapidly changing society. Initially, the focus of the program was on the prevention of substance abuse, including alcohol and tobacco. But the emphasis soon expanded to include adolescents' relationships with peers and their capacity to resist pressures from their peers who rationalize undesirable behavior with the excuse that "everybody does it."

Another important skill to be taught is assertiveness. Some adults may resist this idea because teenagers seem to them all too assertive by nature, expressing themselves forcefully on occasions when the adult view is that what adolescents have to say is, at best, inappropriate. But there are many aspects to assertiveness, and without some command of them, young people are severely handicapped. For example, they should learn how to be assertive in order to take advantage of certain opportunities, such as how to use community resources offered by social and health services. Adolescents also must learn to be assertive in protecting themselves against intimidation by peers without isolating themselves. They must learn to be assertive in resolving conflicts without resort to violence.

Why must all this be taught? Because young adolescents are very easily embarrassed and disappointed when relationships with others, peers as well as adults, go awry. Without training and effective models, their deficient or undeveloped social skills may impel them to defensive aggressiveness, excessively compliant behavior, or painful withdrawal. While disadvantaged youngsters who grow up segregated from the mainstream may be able to acquire the life skills needed in their own neighborhoods, they may lack skills that prepare them for school or work in a different setting. And even young people who are sheltered by the advantages of affluence may lack the skills that will allow them to function successfully in a larger society, especially if their homes have been strained by divorce or other stress.

Many experts find that the best way to teach adolescents how to change their behavior is to make them active agents in bringing about change. Since 1983, Robert Weisberg and his colleagues at Yale University have collaborated with New Haven schools to establish the Yale–New Haven Social Competence Promotion Program for middle school students. At its core are seventeen lessons in social competence. Students take part in role playing, watch live and filmed presentations on how to handle certain situations, join small discussion groups, play competitive and cooperative games, and are provided with a variety of information on the prevention of substance use.

The program addresses itself to emotional situations: how can adolescents learn to recognize and deal with stress without reacting in a destructive manner? It proposes the following steps of behavior: (1) stop, calm down, and think before you act; (2) analyze the problem and your feelings about it; (3) set yourself a goal for action; (4) think of a variety of solutions; (5) consider the consequences of the various options; (6) go ahead and explore what you think is the best plan, and if that plan does not work, try another.

In the New Haven program, inner-city adolescents were asked to describe the stress experienced in their daily lives. They reported physical or verbal aggression they faced; being blamed for something they did not do; strains of establishing closer relationships with others of the same or opposite sex; and the difficulty of living up to teachers' and parents' expectations.

To prepare for leadership in the Yale–New Haven project, classroom teachers take part in five-day summer workshops conducted by Yale faculty and other experienced teachers from the school system. In addition, the prospective teachers attend five two-hour follow-up training sessions and receive on-site coaching during the school year.

Both teachers and students found the program effective.

Teachers responded that the youngsters showed improvement in controlling their impulses, in becoming more sociable, and in performing better academically. The adolescents themselves reported less misbehavior.

Among other promising ways of orienting young people to behavioral hazards and how to avoid them is the use of peer mentoring—that is, providing a model for judicious behavior through the young person's relationship with another who is a sympathetic and experienced adviser. Youthful peer mentors should be supervised by competent adults.

The useful byproduct of peer mentoring is that, in the course of serious discussion, friendships are formed. The most successful examples tend to involve peer counselors who are slightly older and who can guide the young adolescents toward useful activities.

A feeling of being useful gives adolescents a sense of mental and psychological well-being. Many adolescents derive gratification from service to the elderly in nursing homes and hospitals, or from working and playing with young children in day-care centers. The forging of bonds with other members of the community, and particularly across the boundaries of age, helps to expand young people's minds to realize the importance of caring. It is not a sign of selfishness if, in the process, adolescents begin to feel that they, too, are entitled to care and nurture. At the same time, they need to be made to understand their role and responsibility for preventing damage both to themselves and to others.

ADOLESCENTS AS HEALTH-CARE CONSUMERS: FORGING THE LINKS BETWEEN SCHOOL AND HEALTH CENTERS

Because of the great scarcity of health-care facilities for adolescents, attention is increasingly focused on school-based or school-related clinics or centers. Unfortunately, as of 1991, according to the Center for Population Options, there are only 327 such centers in thirty-three states and Puerto

Rico, most of them in urban areas with concentrations of the poor and minorities. These centers perform important functions, and their development must be speeded up dramatically. It is estimated that the existing centers serve no more than 187,000 adolescents, or fewer than 1 percent out of a population of more than 35 million between the ages of ten and nineteen. And while not all or even a majority of adolescents need the services of the centers, the present situation is clearly inadequate. According to the Center for Population Options, more than half of the centers' users have no other source of health care, and in some centers, the proportion of teenagers without access to other health care is nearly 100 percent. Almost 40 percent of the users are completely uninsured.

While 51 percent of the 327 existing centers serve high school students, 13 percent are linked to middle or junior high schools; another 19 percent operate in elementary schools and 12 percent in schools with combined grade levels. Young people appear to show greater confidence in health services linked to the schools — institutions in which they have developed some measure of trust, or at least of familiarity. Many adolescent clients are self-referred, and they probably would not receive any health care if the school-linked center did not exist. In one typical center, 38 percent of the clients reported that they would not have gone elsewhere for care or treatment. Twenty-six percent of those who use school-related centers said that they had no previous source of medical care other than hospital emergency rooms.

Approximately 30 percent of those who visit the centers develop a pattern of regular use. Most of the visits to school-linked centers are for physical examinations, acute illness, and minor emergencies. But it is significant that in the course of such visits mental health problems are often discovered. In four San Francisco centers, for example, between 15 and 36 percent of the young patients were diagnosed to require treatment for mental health problems, even though they had made appointments for other reasons.

While it is too soon to draw any firm conclusions about the

effect of the centers on more positive teenage behavior, some favorable reports are worth noting. In New York City, students who used school-linked centers missed fewer school days than did their classmates who did not make use of the centers. Other centers, however, have reported no such difference in absenteeism. On the other hand, Kansas City centers have reported a significant decline in the number of adolescents who used alcohol and drugs, or smoked, during the two years since the program began: for example, cigarette smoking by adolescent patients dropped from 13 percent to 5 percent, and experimentation with marijuana went down from 31 to 21 percent. These early findings are still far from conclusive, but they give reason for hope that these positive changes are the result of effective counseling by sensitive and knowledgeable health professionals.

Comparing different centers' accomplishments and the background, training, and personality of health-care providers could go a long way toward assuring the success of centers and creating a better understanding of what fails and what succeeds in combatting risk-creating habits. The problem is crucial. Action should not be postponed until further research findings are at hand; even today's limited experience in the field can prevent harm and save lives.

One distressing obstacle remains. Some critics—a vocal minority—oppose school-related health centers in the belief that they encourage and increase teenage sexual activity. Yet, research based on past experience shows that, while the amount of sexual activity does not appear to have been affected one way or the other among young people who use the centers, there is strong indication that the pregnancy rate among them has declined. In Baltimore, according to a 1986 study at Johns Hopkins University, the pregnancy rate declined by 30 percent, compared with a 58 percent increase among students in control groups who did not make use of the centers. Such reports, though still inconclusive, should be considered in the context of the centers' broad purposes, which include, but do not concentrate on, sex-related services.

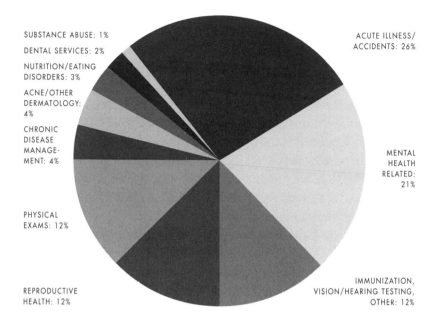

SUBSTANCE ABUSE: 1%

DENTAL SERVICES: 2%

NUTRITION/EATING DISORDERS: 3%

ACNE/OTHER DERMATOLOGY: 4%

CHRONIC DISEASE MANAGEMENT: 4%

PHYSICAL EXAMS: 12%

REPRODUCTIVE HEALTH: 12%

ACUTE ILLNESS/ ACCIDENTS: 26%

MENTAL HEALTH RELATED: 21%

IMMUNIZATION, VISION/HEARING TESTING, OTHER: 12%

Adolescents' Reasons for Visits to School-based Health Centers,[1] 1989–90

PERCENTAGE OF REASONS (FIGURES ROUNDED TO NEAREST WHOLE PERCENTAGE)

Source: J. G. Lear, H. B. Gleicher, A. St. Germaine, and P. J. Porter (1991). "Reorganizing Health Care for Adolescents: The Experience of the School-based Adolescent Health Care Program," *Journal of Adolescent Health* 12: 450–58.

[1] 13,000 patient visits (22 percent of total visits) not reported by primary diagnosis or service.

Almost without exception, health centers have been opened without local conflict, suggesting general community acceptance. And more than 90 percent of parents who gave permission to their children to use the centers have chosen not to limit the services they could receive.

Because American institutional memory is short, remedies for social ills must be reinvented periodically, and school-related health services are no exception. The first such care system was established around 1890 to deal with the large numbers of immigrant children who were arriving in the United States with infectious diseases. In 1892, New York City initiated such a care system. Physicians visited schools to teach hygiene and other means of preventing illness. When money ran out and the medical establishment, afraid of competition, turned against the free service (some private physicians even today oppose school-related centers for the same reason), the position of school nurse was invented. By 1980, schools employed 45,000 school nurses. But while the nurses kept health records and provided first aid, medical treatment still remained the virtual monopoly of private physicians.

During the 1960s, largely in response to highly visible numbers of homeless, vagrant, and often drug-abusing young people, community-based health-service stations, such as the Haight-Ashbury Free Clinic and The DOOR, were established to provide one-stop, free, and confidential services. In 1967, the Cambridge, Massachusetts, health department began providing medical services to school children at a clinic in an elementary school.

The first modern school-linked clinic was established in 1970, in West Dallas, Texas, as part of a project by the Department of Pediatrics at the University of Texas Health Sciences Center. It did not offer reproductive health services. The first school-linked center to provide comprehensive services, including family planning and prenatal care, was established in 1973 in St. Paul, Minnesota. In an effort to keep teenagers in school after they gave birth, it also offered child care.

In 1987, a number of school-based health centers were opened with support from the Robert Wood Johnson Foundation. (The foundation made grants in eleven states and fourteen cities.) In their third year, the centers reported that 71 percent of the schools' students had their parents' permission to use the facilities. Black students used the centers more than any other group—57 percent in 1989–90, compared to 28 percent for Hispanics and 20 percent for whites.

Treating acute illness and injury remain the centers' leading services, constituting 26 percent of the total, followed by mental health-related care, including individual and group therapy, with 21 percent.

What gives the school-related service for adolescents its special character and mission is that it treats a population that is distinct in its needs both from children, who typically suffer from infectious diseases, and from adults with such chronic illnesses as cancer and heart problems. The threats to adolescents' health tend, instead, to be caused by accidents, homicide, suicide, substance abuse, and unprotected sexual activity.

The most constructive approach to adolescent health is the promotion of behavior that prevents poor health, both now and in the future. Therefore, a special focus should be on encouraging sound nutrition, sensible exercise, and the avoidance of addictive and dangerous substances and on providing the foundation for a sensitive moral and physical approach to health, including sexuality. This perspective calls for actively preventing mental disorders, in part through education about the causes of depression and alienation. The adolescent process of moving from childlike dependence to adult independence has never been as fraught with risks as it is today; it creates stress and conflict, which can undermine mental stability. Guiding even the most sheltered and stable adolescent to a healthy transition requires sensitivity as youngsters revise old relationships, including those with their parents, and as they begin to form new and constructive bonds. Those who are struggling with the liabilities of poverty and racial discrimination or live in a stressful home environment need even greater support as they prepare for an uncertain future.

In responding to the need for diagnosis, help, and support, school-related health centers bear a special burden: a great deal is expected of them because they are considered part of the education system and therefore presumed to have a particular understanding of young people and their problems. In a way, these centers are asked to perform miracles in a field in which many of the traditional health delivery systems perform poorly or not at all. The danger is that by being judged against unrealistic standards, school-related services may be prematurely pronounced failures and consequently starved of funds or abandoned altogether.

One of the questions still to be explored is that of the centers' location. Should they be on school grounds, adjacent to schools, or at a more distant site—possibly serving more than one school? The advantages of centers located at or near schools is that they are convenient for the students, making it more likely that they will keep their appointments for follow-up visits. The disadvantages of locating the centers on school grounds are that they may be less accessible to out-of-school youths, that their services may be limited to school hours, and that they may be closed during vacation time.

On what kinds of services should the centers concentrate? Should they be acting primarily as first-aid stations, chiefly dealing with crises such as sudden acute illness or accidents? Or should they offer preventive care and long-range health promotion? In practice, their choices may be limited: they are likely to be guided by clients' demands. Surely, they cannot ignore crises as they arise. But, in view of the great extent of young adolescents' needs for preventive as well as acute health services, it makes no sense not to take a broad view of the centers' mission, and this is to serve as an educational and diagnostic tool for the preservation of young people's well-being and for the prevention of damage to their minds and bodies.

Most centers offer both "drop-in" care and scheduled appointments. They tend to operate during regular school hours, although a few are open in the evening and on weekends. Limits on funding force most of them to close during the summer vacation months—a serious disadvantage, since this is the time when many adolescents need health care and counseling.

Existing clinics provide assessment of health problems and treatment of minor injuries, and some aspects of health education. Dental services are provided by only about 35 percent of the centers. More than 85 percent offer laboratory tests, physical examinations for general and sports purposes, some medication, referrals to community health agencies or to local physicians, counseling, referrals for pregnancy cases, and guidance on nutrition, weight control, and mental health.

Between 60 and 85 percent of the existing school-linked centers provide gynecological examinations, diagnosis, treatment of sexually transmitted diseases, immunization, sex education classes, substance abuse education programs, and education about parenting. Only 28 percent write prescriptions for birth control pills, and fewer than 20 percent dispense any kind of contraceptives.

As a result of the recent controversy about whether acknowledging adolescent sexual activity means encouraging it, health centers are less likely to prescribe contraceptives. This is paradoxical indeed; for while abstinence from sexual activity certainly is the best way for adolescents to protect themselves against AIDS and other sexually transmitted diseases, the tragic growth of AIDS among young people makes it imperative that those who engage in sexual activity be supplied with condoms. A 1991 Roper poll found that 64 percent of Americans endorse condom distribution in high schools.

The centers can be a useful link between their own medically oriented function and the new educational mission of schools that plan to introduce human biology as the core of science instruction for young adolescents. (For details, see chapter 3.) One important goal in teaching human biology is to encourage students to consider their existing and potential health problems and to acquire expertise in disease prevention. Such knowledge is particularly important in helping youngsters to make positive decisions concerning the use of alcohol, cigarettes, and drugs; to consider matters of diet and exercise; and to deal with their sexual behavior. All of these considerations run parallel to the services offered by school-related centers.

This connection between classroom and center could greatly expand the school's relevance to adolescents without in any way reducing its capacity for intellectual development. But the connection will also pose a test for school staffs. A sympathetic and health-conscious principal is essential to avoid friction. School personnel might be invited to serve on the health centers' advisory boards. Since many schools employ a school nurse, she or he could be a coordinator between the two institutions.

A realistic analysis of the relationship between schools and health centers should nevertheless alert planners to potential resentment by some staff members. Even though the schools' traditional health services are inadequate—if they exist at all beyond some cursory classroom instruction—some administrators and teachers may regard health center personnel as intruders on their turf. And since school people feel continually under-funded, they may also begrudge the centers' access to public funds, even if the money does not come out of school budgets. Educators should be aware that most school-linked health centers are operated by agencies other than the schools themselves, which include hospitals, medical schools, community health centers, and local health departments. Much of their funding comes from the federal government's Maternal and Child Health Block Grant.

Other conflicts must be avoided. Despite school guidance counselors' persistent and often justified complaints that they are overworked and therefore are unable to give students more than cursory attention, they may perceive the arrival of a new institution on their territory as a threat to their authority and even security. Even though the medical profession in general appears to favor school-linked health centers, some physicians still oppose them. In efforts to protect turf and income, some private physicians see the centers as a threat to their authority and profits.

Diplomacy is needed. Joint planning from the very start can

do much to turn competition into cooperation. Equally important is a close and friendly relationship between the centers and the existing community services, the voluntary organizations, the religious organizations, and private physicians. Past and continuing deficiencies in health services for youth should leave no doubt that all hands are needed to build a comprehensive system of prevention and care. The long waiting lists at the existing centers of teenagers whose physical and mental health problems ought to be given instant attention should dispel any doubt about the need to build a comprehensive network that can reduce the harm done by blocked or delayed access.

Parents should, of course, be natural partners in the development of centers intended to watch over and improve adolescents' health. Unfortunately, parents tend to be least available in poor communities where parental need is the greatest. After a day of exhausting labor, parents often lack the time and energy to take on another responsibility. Often, too, they distrust the schools as seats of governmental and bureaucratic power and look on them with an exasperated sense of their own powerlessness. Yet, even in the face of such distrust, once the centers are available, most parents urge their children to make use of them.

At this early point in the school-linked centers' existence, parents seem to be generally supportive and adolescents are "voting with their feet" by turning to the centers for help and advice.

An example of effective school-based centers is the health center at Franklin K. Lane High School in Queens, New York, which began full operations early in 1991. Its staff includes two part-time physicians, several nurses, a pediatric nurse-practitioner, a clinical nurse specialist in mental health, and a coordinator–health educator.

Ronald Shenker, chief of the Division of Adolescent Medicine at Schneider Children's Hospital in New Hyde Park, New York, is codirector of the center. He says that, while the 4,500-student school is in a "nice lower middle-class, multiethnic area," its population comes from "a community where there are not a lot of private practitioners. Medical care is episodic, emergency-room, out of the mainstream of private practice."

Many of the school's adolescents suffer from chronic diseases, such as asthma and diabetes, or nutritional deficiencies. Many have problems related to adolescent sexuality or have contracted sexually transmitted diseases. There are many unwanted pregnancies.

Shenker estimates that 20 percent of the students are eligible for Medicaid reimbursement, but all students who have parental permission to use the clinic are treated. "Nobody pays out of pocket," Shenker says. While the center is open to all students, it cannot routinely take care of the entire enrollment; it therefore targets the ninth grade.

"We see quite a number of kids with emotional problems, and we find a high incidence of mental illness," says Martha Arden, who is an associate professor of pediatrics at Schneider Hospital and spends 60 percent of her time at the school's center. In some cases, the physicians say, even parents who could afford it would not seek medical care for their children, perhaps because they prefer not to acknowledge that their children show signs of mental illness.

José Cárdenas, a psychologist in the Teen Health Center at San Fernando (California) High School, where he himself was once a student, works hard at improving the mental health of teenagers who have been sexually abused. After joining the center in 1987, he learned that the problems of many girls and some boys who had difficulty in establishing relationships with their peers and who had attempted suicide, or who had early pregnancies or paternities, could be traced to their own prior sexual abuse. At least one year of psychotherapy, often without the parents' knowledge, aims at convincing the students that they are not "damaged goods"—that they are not condemned to being victims.

David Kaplan, chief of adolescent medicine at the University of Colorado School of Medicine in Denver, reports: "It's not unusual for us to find a teenager who comes into the school-based clinic and, finally, the fact will come out that he's been kicked out of the house, for any of a number of reasons, and has been moving around from one friend's house to another for two weeks. It's hard for a kid like that to think about his future in a way that makes him want to stay in school and graduate. We try to help them with that."

The Denver experience underscores the potential of school-based centers. Approximately 70 percent of the schools' students are enrolled in the city's three centers. In 1990, more than 4,000 visits were logged for 1,600 students. Kaplan estimates that about 25 percent of the students in each school have no health insurance.

Despite some rave reviews from physicians and the centers' obvious usefulness, school-related centers still face serious obstacles: money is scarce, and funding often seems to fall between education and health budgets, both already under great pressure; solid scientific evidence of their effectiveness must await a longer period of operation; and, perhaps most serious of all, ideological and religious opposition continues to focus on the centers' sex-related services. Yet, to eliminate or curtail such services would cripple the centers' capacity to treat adolescent health.

This would be a serious blow to teenage health development. Recent reports from California show that between 11 and 44 percent of those adolescents who have begun to use school-linked centers have not had any contact with health providers during the previous two to three years. In New York State, it is estimated that 42 percent of its children, including adolescents, are too poor to get adequate health care or any care at all.

The general record of dental care is equally disconcerting. Almost 10 percent of youths from poor or low-income homes have never been seen by a dentist, and nearly half do not see a dentist annually.

A further question about the quality of health care and preventive medical guidance is raised by the fact that, when adolescents do consult physicians, short visits lasting less than eleven minutes are more common for them than for any other age group. This is particularly distressing when we consider that, in 1986, the Office of Technology Assessment estimated that at least 12 percent of the nation's children and young adolescents were in need of some mental health treatment—fewer than one-third of them had received it. Throughout the country, mental health services for adolescents often have long waiting lists.

Whether the temptation to which any adolescent succumbs is drug or alcohol abuse, cigarette smoking, the reckless use of automobiles, or thoughtless and dangerous sexual activity, the result is intolerably costly in human suffering and money. The challenge is to enlist all available resources of the home, the school, the health profession, the community, and the religious organizations to reduce the risks. Just as the prevention of conflict in the conduct of a nation's foreign policy is infinitely preferable to war, so it is far better to prevent damage to adolescent health than to battle the consequences of ignorance and neglect.

CHAPTER THREE

BABIES BORN TO CHILDREN

ADOLESCENT SEX AND HEALTH

t sounded like a horror story. A new-born baby, alive and screaming, was found by two city sanitation workers in the garbage disposal chute of a Brooklyn, New York, housing project. Investigation led to a twelve-year-old girl who had given birth secretly and, in her panic, had tried to get rid of the baby when the time came for her to leave for school. The public was shocked almost to disbelief. How could a twelve-year-old child be a mother? Who was the responsible male? How could a baby be treated, literally, as garbage?

The answers to those questions make the story no less horrible and, tragically, only too real. Twelve-year-olds giving birth is no longer a rarity in the United States. The baby's father was the girl's adult cousin. Incest, seduction, and the rape of children by adult members of families occurs more often than our society is ready to admit.

The consequences? The father was arrested, the disposition of his case uncertain. The adolescent mother is in one foster home, the baby in another. Both are likely to become long-term victims of a foster-care system already in shambles. The human tragedy continues.

Human tragedies, however, come in many forms; rarely are they given the kind of attention that the rescued baby of Brooklyn received. Still, early adolescent pregnancies are almost always tragic events. Their prevention should be given highest

priority, not only for the sake of the mothers and the babies, but for the future of society as well. "I was hurt because it was a baby having a baby," said a woman neighbor of the twelve-year-old. She knew too well that such births create a new generation of children who are deprived of the benefits of nurture by a mature parent and a supportive family. About 10,000 adolescents under the age of fifteen annually give birth in the United States.

Local surveys indicate that the average age of first intercourse in some inner cities is much lower than it is nationally. Judith Jones, director of Columbia University's National Center for Children in Poverty, reports that in the Washington Heights area of Manhattan, "it is not unusual for eleven-year-old boys and girls to 'make out'; with mother at work, there are plenty of opportunities right at home. . . . Junior high school personnel have described 'catching students doing it' in hallways, bathrooms and locker rooms."

The rate of births among American teenagers is unmatched in the rest of the industrial world. The percentage of unmarried teenage mothers has risen steadily over the past several decades. In 1984, it was more than three times what it had been twenty-five years earlier. Based on statistics released by the National Research Council in 1985, the annual cost in public funds for teenage pregnancies is between $15 billion and $18 billion. Of all mothers under the age of thirty who receive Aid to Families with Dependent Children, 71 percent began their childbearing as teenagers.

The average age of first intercourse of American teenagers is 16.2 for girls and 15.7 for boys. Approximately one-fourth of fifteen-year-old girls and one-third of fifteen-year-old boys have had sexual intercourse. (According to a recent survey, by age fifteen 13 percent of white boys and 6 percent of white girls have had intercourse, compared to 45 percent of black boys and 10 percent of black girls.) More than one-fifth of all first premarital pregnancies happen in the month after "the first time," and half occur within six months. Three-fourths of all unintended teenage pregnancies happen to adolescents who do not use contraception.

These realities take on a special sense of urgency when we consider that, among sexually active girls of fifteen to nineteen, about 15 percent have never used contraception, and more than 50 percent have not used it at first intercourse. More than 75 percent of Hispanic and 66 percent of black young women, compared to 45 percent of white young women, did not use any protection the first time they had intercourse. While adolescents are more likely than other groups to report that they used condoms or withdrawal at first intercourse, almost one-third of all sexually active adolescents continue to have sexual intercourse without using any birth control devices whatsoever.

U.S. birthrates for white teenagers alone are higher than those for teenagers in any other Western country; the figures for black American teenagers are three times the rate for whites. American girls under age eighteen have proportionately twice as many babies as British and Canadian girls, more than three times as many as the French, and more than four times as many as the Swedish and the Dutch.

When asked why Dutch rates are so relatively low, Dutch sociologist Evert Ketting replied: "We in Holland don't think of our rates as low. We would like to see them drop even further. What amazes me is how high rates are in the United States. How can the richest country in the world allow a situation to continue that would not be tolerated in other countries?"

While the public focus tends to be on adolescents who choose to engage in early sex, substantial (but as yet uncounted) numbers of girls experience their first intercourse involuntarily as victims of rape and incest. A small sample survey found that almost one-third of sexually active respondents had had unwanted sexual encounters. Sexual child abuse is believed to be far more widespread than the number of cases that come to light in the courts would suggest. In addition, many girls consent to early sex under peer pressure or because they believe they have no other way of engaging and holding a boy's attention. Many young adolescents are impregnated, not by teenagers, but by adult males.

In her book, *Within Our Reach*, Lisbeth B. Schorr recounts the story of one teenager, Sherita. Sherita had told a *Washington Post* reporter that she and her boyfriend began having sex when she was eleven and he was twelve. At fifteen, she became afraid of losing him and decided to become pregnant in the hope of "holding on to him."

In another account, fifteen-year-old Mary, a ninth-grader in Chicago, first had intercourse the week she was suspended from school as punishment for chronic truancy. (It seems an odd punishment indeed for truants to be forced to legitimize their truancy through suspension.) Mary had not been sure she wanted to "go all the way" with her sixteen-year-old boyfriend, but he put pressure on her. She believed she could not get pregnant the first time she had sexual intercourse, so she gave in. About six weeks later Mary began to worry about her period and went to a family planning clinic for contraceptive advice. She had come too late. She was pregnant. "Her story," says Schorr, "of ignorance and confusion, of intercourse too early, and a clinic visit too late has been repeated, in its essentials, hundreds of thousands of times."

The direct impact of early adolescent sexual activity is amply documented. In 1988, approximately 2.5 million adolescents had a sexually transmitted disease; an estimated one-quarter of them were infected before graduating from high school. According to the American Medical Association, gonorrhea rates are actually higher among sexually active fifteen- to nineteen-year-olds than among young adults between the ages of twenty and twenty-four.

Today, the risk of AIDS makes preventive measures of paramount importance. In 1988, more than 50 percent of all fifteen- to nineteen-year-olds reported having had sexual intercourse within the past three months, but only 22 percent of the sexually active females in that age group reported that they were currently using condoms, which aside from abstinence is the only relatively safe protection against contracting AIDS.

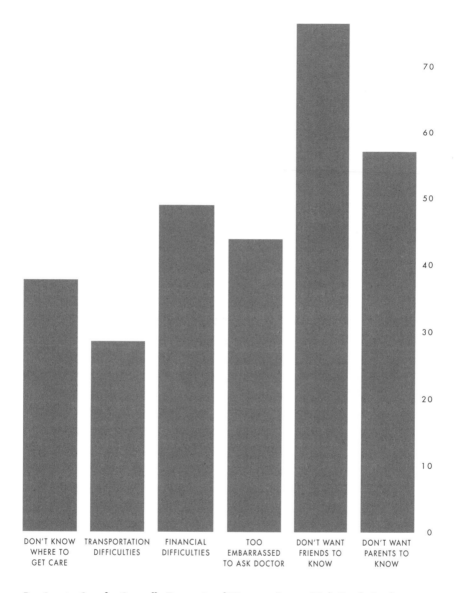

70

60

50

40

30

20

10

0

DON'T KNOW WHERE TO GET CARE   TRANSPORTATION DIFFICULTIES   FINANCIAL DIFFICULTIES   TOO EMBARRASSED TO ASK DOCTOR   DON'T WANT FRIENDS TO KNOW   DON'T WANT PARENTS TO KNOW

Barriers to Care for Sexually Transmitted Diseases Among 10th-Grade Students

PERCENTAGE OF STUDENTS

Source: American School Health Association, Association for the Advancement of Health Education, and Society for Public Health Education, Inc. (1989). *The National Adolescent Student Health Survey: A Report on the Health of America's Youth.* Oakland, California.

THE DIMENSIONS AND CONSEQUENCES
OF ADOLESCENT PREGNANCY

A part from the high risk of disease, the increase of sexual activity among young girls is creating monumental social problems. Early, usually unwanted, pregnancies are placing the future lives of great numbers of teenage girls in jeopardy, interrupting, and often terminating, their education and drastically reducing their job and career opportunities. Despite dropout prevention programs and special counseling efforts to help pregnant girls stay in school, or to return to school after their babies are born, the majority still leave school.

Statistically, the younger a girl is at first intercourse, the less likely she is to use contraception, the earlier she bears her first child, and the more children she will have. The failure to use contraception becomes even more troubling because it is often the male partner who decides whether or not a contraceptive will be used. And when a girl becomes pregnant, the male frequently decides whether or not she will carry the baby to term.

Currently, one in six babies born in the United States is born to a school-age mother. There are 1.3 million children living with teenage mothers—half of them unmarried. Another 6 million children under the age of five are living with mothers who were adolescents when they gave birth.

The damage that results from the birth of children to children is not confined to the young mother; it often has long-term adverse effects on the baby. Risks include low birth weight, abnormalities related to inadequate prenatal care, and child abuse. Evidence suggests that when these children reach school age, they frequently do poorly, have serious behavioral and emotional problems, and are at high risk of becoming teenage parents themselves, remaining imprisoned in lives of poverty with all its devastating consequences.

As is so often the case, minority status increases the burdens. The National Research Council reports that, by age seven, white children of adolescent mothers show no behavioral differences from children of older mothers, but black youngsters, especially boys, experience problems in social behavior. Both boys and girls of black adolescent mothers tend to have more behavioral problems than do children of older black mothers, which is probably a reflection of the young mothers' immaturity and lack of understanding about how to be an effective parent. Girls of black adolescent mothers exhibit more bed-wetting and phobias, for example; boys show more thumb-sucking and speech deficiencies.

Generally, children of black adolescents are found to be at greater risk over time in terms of reduced capacity for learning and overall intellectual development. Boys' maladjustment is often expressed as rebelliousness, aggression, and the inability to control anger; girls tend to show fearfulness. During the adolescent years from age twelve to seventeen, these youngsters develop more mental problems than do children of older mothers; girls are likely to be more aggressive, more impulsive, more emotional, and unable to form sound relationships with peers.

As a group, children born of adolescent mothers suffer academically, emotionally, and economically, and they tend to fall seriously behind those children born to women in their twenties who have similar backgrounds. They are more likely to have children during adolescence; their dropout rate is higher; their school performance is worse; they become sexually active earlier than their peers; they are more likely to encounter trouble with school discipline; they run away from home more often; they have more problems with drugs and alcohol; and they are prone to inflict injury on others.

The adolescent mothers at highest risk are in their early teens, black, poor, and insufficiently nourished. They either have ignored the need for prenatal care or have had no ready access to it. As a result of these conditions, the infant is likely to be premature and too small to thrive and, particularly when the mother has been using drugs, alcohol, or cigarettes, born with serious physical and mental defects. The mother herself is at high risk of being abandoned by the baby's father; of facing a lifetime of unemployment or low-paying jobs; of living in a home without a stable family; and of experiencing persistent health problems. Moreover, the single mother usually has to do the work of mother and father, except in extended family situations, resulting in survival at a most modest level of subsistence.

In its working paper *Risking the Future: Adolescent Sexuality, Pregnancy, and Childbearing,* the National Research Council cites "evidence of some important differences in attitudes between blacks and whites." It reports that blacks appear to have greater tolerance for sexual activity outside marriage than have whites and that black neighborhoods demonstrate a greater tolerance for out-of-wedlock births. It is interesting to note that, in elementary school, black boys and girls have attitudes about childbearing that are similar to those of whites—that having children should come after marriage—but that as they grow older these attitudes appear to change.

Most available studies show that early sexual experience is linked to a low level of education, with both adolescent mothers and their youngsters suffering from spotty school attendance and, consequently, high dropout rates.

Under current economic conditions, dropping out of school disastrously affects a young person's long-term income and job opportunities. Adult self-sufficiency may be an almost impossible goal: a poorly educated school-age mother who has to cope with one or more babies will earn less than half of the income of young women who have not dropped out of school and have become mothers later. The school-age mother's chances of earning enough to support herself and her child are slim, and since most of the men she comes into contact with are also likely to be economically disadvantaged as a result of having little education and few job skills, she may not have the opportunity or the incentive to marry.

In 1987, according to the Alan Guttmacher Institute, some 1,014,000 teenagers became pregnant. About 31,000 were younger than fifteen. Of all pregnant teenagers, 50 percent gave birth, 36 percent had abortions, and 14 percent had miscarriages. The latest statistics, reported by the federal Centers for

Disease Control in August 1991, show a small increase in the rate at which pregnant teenagers are giving birth.

Who are the young people most likely to engage in sexual intercourse at an early age? The composite picture that emerges is one of young adolescents of low-income families with poorly educated parents who establish little communication with their children. It should be noted, however, that rates of early sexual activity are up among all socioeconomic and ethnic groups.

Engaging in early, and usually unprotected, sex is frequently linked with the teenagers' lack of interest and poor performance in school. Perhaps partly because they may have little self-esteem or expectations of a successful future, they may be truants. They may be living in a racially or ethnically segregated community, surrounded by poverty and adult unemployment, and they translate what they see among adults as a reliable forecast of what their own lives are likely to be. These youngsters move in circles of friends with similar liabilities. Studies tell us that these teens who engage in early sexual activity often use alcohol or other drugs such as marijuana, cocaine, or amphetamines.

The home life of these young adolescents tends to be dismal. Many lack the presence, or knowledge, of a father. Their mother may engage in sex with one or more partners, without concealing the sexual activity from the young people in the home. Many of the adult males with whom these adolescents come in contact engage in sexual activities irresponsibly and without concern for their sexual partner's feelings.

Across the social and economic spectrum, part of the problem of teenage pregnancy is caused by adolescents' identifying with romantic media images that portray a pleasurable uncontrollable surrender to the passion of the moment. In any case, neither the girl nor the boy is "prepared" for "it" to happen. Adolescents tend to be highly ignorant about when conception occurs. The same old myths stand in the way of effective birth control: "It can't happen the first time." "You can't get pregnant standing up." "Douching after sex will keep you from getting pregnant."

PREVENTING ADOLESCENT PREGNANCY: THE ISSUES

The National Research Council's panel on Adolescent Pregnancy and Childbearing urges that the highest priority be given to the problem of early, unwanted pregnancies for both humane and economic reasons. It is far less costly to prevent problems than it is to struggle with their consequences, particularly when those consequences carry with them multigenerational repercussions that have the most dangerous implications for all of society. The effect on the quality of young people's lives and, in fact, all lives is immense. Maryland's Department of Health and Mental Hygiene found, for example, that every dollar that goes to family planning services for females under age twenty saves $3.50 of federal and state funds. Savings are also realized in the budgets of state agencies that serve adolescents who become pregnant.

How can we effect change? Clearly, it is preferable for teenagers to postpone their sexual activity. Every effort should be made to teach them strategies to overcome peer pressure to have sex. This includes age-appropriate information on human sexuality that stresses the advantages of being equipped to build a well-ordered and mature family life.

Help must also come from role models. Young people require strong cultural and social support from caring adults. They need to see more ethnically diverse, positive depictions of adults in the media. Sexually active adolescents must learn the facts about birth control and use it consistently. The National Research Council considers the contraceptive pill to be the safest and most effective means of birth control for sexually active adolescents and urges professionals to dispel myths about its risks to young users. A new contraceptive, Norplant, which is implanted in the arm, may turn out to be a good contraceptive for sexually active teens, but there have been no studies published of its use with this population group. Concern about the threat of AIDS should give new priority to the use of condoms accompanied by a spermicide as the best available device for protection against both sexually transmitted diseases and pregnancy. Still, obstacles remain. For example, Holley Galland reported in a 1991 *Journal of the American Medical Association* that the state-approved curriculum for AIDS education in Louisiana "is not allowed to mention the word condom."

When prevention fails, early parenthood is not the only available choice. For young people who are unwilling to give birth, or unable or unwilling to assume the responsibilities of parenthood, three possibilities exist: abortion, adoption, and foster care. The National Research Council calls for abortion to be available as one option for pregnant adolescent girls. Yet, even that option is now at risk as the courts contemplate limiting its availability.

As for foster care, Robert Ayasse, a social worker in Contra Costa County, California, asks us to imagine that we are sticking a piece of tape on a surface, pulling it up, then pressing it down, pulling it up again and pressing it down again, and keeping up the process over and over again. Soon the tape will lose its ability to adhere. Ayasse, who counsels foster children in four California school districts, explains that his metaphor depicts what happens to many foster children who are "pulled up" and shifted from one foster home to another again and again. Many of these youngsters have trouble developing and sustaining emotional attachments and succeeding in school. In many instances, children are referred to foster homes after they have been subjected to abuse. Some foster homes may perpetuate such physical or sexual mistreatment, but even in homes that provide good care, attempting to overcome prior harmful treatment requires devoted effort not often found in homes where emotional and/or financial resources are strained.

When pregnant teenagers opt for abortion, many localities require that they obtain parental consent. Even in this era of disappearing taboos, the statement "If my parents find out, they'll kill me" is a familiar response to counselors who assist pregnant teenagers of every social class. A young adolescent's right to privacy and confidentiality is often the crucial issue on which she bases her decision about whether or not to give birth. Because adolescents are so reluctant to seek care for sex-related problems and behavior in the first place, they need access to reproductive advice and health care on a confidential basis.

Yet, the issue of confidentiality and parental notification causes the most heated debate. The Center for Population Options puts it this way: "When a teenager is having sex, the desire for confidentiality is compelling. When a teenager is pregnant, her desire for privacy is extreme. Still, not every teenager clings so fiercely to familial privacy. In fact, the majority of adolescents choose to involve a parent voluntarily in pregnancy outcome decisions. But for those who feel they cannot involve their parents, a law forcing that communication merely increases the obstacles to a safe outcome."

One tragic example of how the lack of confidentiality can affect the lives of young people is the story about a twelve-year-old pregnant girl from Idaho named Spring Adams. Spring, the victim of incest, had arranged to have an out-of-state abortion to avoid having her father notified. At the last moment her father found out about the planned abortion. He shot and killed her. Then he shot himself.

There is much evidence that statutes requiring parental consent tend to cause teenagers who are reluctant to confide in their parents to delay their decision, thus increasing risks to their health by turning to abortion in the second trimester of their pregnancy. On the other hand, competent early abortions present no greater risk for teenagers than they do for adult women.

The controversy over parental notification or consent underscores a more fundamental flaw in the relationship between parents and teenagers in matters of sexuality. If earlier, long-term communication had been established between teenage girls and their parents about sexual attitudes and behavior, including the discussion of the advantages of abstinence and, failing that, contraception, the crisis over pregnancy and the decision concerning abortion might not arise. Grappling with an unwanted pregnancy in an atmosphere of crisis and recrimination is, undoubtedly, the worst way of addressing the sensitive questions that will so dramatically affect the young adolescent and her family.

Confidentiality is vital not only in the matter of pregnancy but also for the diagnosis and treatment of sexually transmitted diseases. Title X of the federal Public Health Services Act provides funds to family planning clinics that serve more than a million teenagers each year. In addition to pregnancy testing, these clinics provide regular screening for sexually transmitted diseases and cancer; they also provide contraceptive counseling. For many poor people of all ages, the clinics are the only source of health care available.

These issues have been further complicated by the U.S. Supreme Court ruling in *Rust v. Sullivan*, which, if ultimately enforced, would prohibit Title X family planning clinics that receive federal dollars from counseling women about their abortion rights—and even from mentioning abortion as an option. Writing in the Letters page of the *New York Times* (July 11, 1991), four counselors in New York City who are regularly consulted by pregnant women age twelve to twenty-one commented: "These are women who are in satisfying relationships, as well as women who have been raped and who are victims of incest. However, these women have one thing in common, they depend on our federally funded Title X health centers to meet their family planning needs.

"We provide health information, including birth-control methods, to enable these young women to take responsibility for their reproductive health. Abortion is a legal medical alternative for all pregnant women; it never is discussed as a method of birth control. . . .

"We hear young women talk about suicide as an alternative to pregnancy and delivery. We hear young women, themselves chronically ill, contemplate the possibility of a deformed fetus. The gag rule [a rule that would prevent counselors or physicians from discussing or answering questions about abortion] tells young women like these they do not deserve to know all their legal medical options because they cannot afford a private physician. . . . "

The Center for Population Options concludes: "Parental consent laws give these parents hope that they will still be able to exercise some control. In reality, these laws do not give parents that control. What they do is potentially pose a fundamental conflict of interest that pits the health and safety of a pregnant girl against the state's insistence that parents be part of the decision." The added risk is that the pregnant teenager will choose a course that may threaten her health and possibly even her life.

Nevertheless, the question of whether parents should be notified before an abortion is performed on the teenager remains intensely controversial. In 1990, the U.S. Supreme Court ruled in two cases involving notification (*Hodgson v. Minnesota* and *Ohio v. Akron Center for Reproductive Health*). In these cases, the court decided that states are allowed to enforce laws requiring notice to one or two parents as long as a judicial "bypass" procedure is in place. Part of an earlier ruling (*Bellotti v. Baird*) requires that the pregnant minor must be entitled to bypass parental consent with a petition for approval of abortion by a judge. Critics of this rule maintain that the procedure is of little help to teenagers who lack the sophistication, the information, and possibly the cash to seek such judicial action.

In a dissenting opinion in the Ohio ruling, Justice Blackmun recognized the dangers of legislating parental notification in pregnancy cases: "For too many young pregnant women, parental involvement in this most intimate decision threatens harm, rather than promises comfort. The court's selective blindness to this stark social reality is bewildering and distressing." Nevertheless, as of 1990, thirty-two states had passed parental notification or consent laws.

Supporters of abortion rights generally agree with opponents of abortion that it would be best if society had no need at all for abortion. The real disagreement, then, is about the ways of reducing its need. While the opponents of abortion rights stress abstinence as the solution, abortion rights supporters maintain that, while abstinence is desirable, the practical way to reduce the demand for abortion is to provide all young people with family planning services, including the availability of birth control.

The Alan Guttmacher Institute observes that these opposing points of view are also reflected in actions taken by the states. For example, Maryland formed a coalition to promote increased expenditures for family planning in an effort to reduce the number of abortions. Legislators and private organizations on both sides of the abortion debate joined forces to ask the state's governor for a $3.2 million budget for family planning services.

At the opposite end of the spectrum, Missouri recommends that "state legislators insure that public funds are not used to promote contraception, sterilization and abortion among teenagers" and instead advocates chastity. The state suggests a system of counselors to "help teens discover the reasons they are sexually active at a young age and help them resolve the basic problems and cope with current difficulties." Utah follows the same line. It does not "support the use of contraception as an alternative for abstinence for teenagers" because, the authorities believe, promoting the use of contraceptives "conveys a message of implied societal approval of sexual intercourse among teenagers."

Sixteen states and the District of Columbia recommend family planning services at some level. Wyoming set the specific goal that, by 1992, 95 percent of its youths who request family planning advice will be able to get it with "reasonable" ease. Only eight states (Colorado, Connecticut, Maine, New York, Texas, Vermont, Wisconsin, and Wyoming) explicitly endorse confidential services. Vermont specifically recommends that "sexually active teenagers have access, without barriers, to contraceptive counseling and services" and suggests continuing education for physicians in adolescent medicine.

Even the Alan Guttmacher Institute, with its long years of

research and activity in the field, admits that "nobody knows how to 'solve' the problem of teenage pregnancy." But it points to Maine's and Connecticut's initiatives as the most comprehensive. Maine is involved in all aspects of teenage pregnancy. It emphasizes prevention but also gives careful consideration to pregnancy options and the promotion of positive outcomes of childbearing. Moreover, it includes recommendations for the involvement of the clergy, the families, and the medical profession as well as the local communities and government agencies.

Whatever a teenager's personal situation in regard to matters of sexuality and reproduction, the least to be expected is that adults respond to the human dilemma in a humane and understanding fashion. The National Research Council's panel on Adolescent Sexuality, Pregnancy, and Childbearing put it into simple words: "At each step along the path from sexual initiation to parenting—regardless of whether one might wish that step had not been reached—the girl or woman should be treated with the same dignity, confidentiality, kindness, and excellence of health care that are due any patient."

Pregnant teenagers who decide to carry their pregnancy to term should be assured early and regular prenatal care and nutrition. Studies show that teenage mothers in the United States have higher rates of severe anemia, pregnancy toxemia, labor and delivery complications, and high morbidity rates. Their babies should be given regular pediatric care from the time of their birth. As for the young mother, every effort should be made to prevent subsequent unintended births that would aggravate all the difficult problems faced by adolescent parents. The National Research Council report found that 30 percent of adolescents who give birth will again be pregnant within two years. Eleven states and the District of Columbia specifically recommend strategies to combat repeat pregnancies, although these are often limited to providing education rather than social services.

Those who would reduce the number of adolescent pregnancies must face the fact that not all such births are unwanted. Many poor girls are convinced that having a baby will give them someone to love and, in return, to be loved by. Having so little satisfaction themselves, and despairing of ever owning something of value, the prospect of creating a new life that belongs to them seems romantic and appealing. In some instances, it may also be a way of "getting back" at their parents or other adults—"to show them" that they are able to take matters into their own hands and to forget their deprivations.

Such dreams of love and power usually overlook the realities of motherhood: its daily responsibilities, including the constant need for money, for time, and the growing conflict between the young mother's own need to develop and the baby's unrelenting need for care and attention. When mother and child are both struggling to grow up, both lives are at risk of being stunted. And the squalid environment from which the teenager had hoped, in some miraculous way, to escape through motherhood remains, now damaging not only the adolescent mother but the infant as well.

And what about the young mother's sexual partner? The National Research Council's panel stressed that it is counterproductive to treat adolescent pregnancy as merely a problem for adolescent girls: males must be taught to be sexually responsible. Their attitude and behavior must be viewed as central to any improvement of present conditions. There are some small encouraging signs. Several studies of unmarried adolescent fathers show "a surprising amount of paternal involvement for extended periods following the birth."

But the overall picture remains grim. In most instances, neither the girl nor the boy has given serious thought to whether the baby will, or ought to, be brought up by a mother and father.

In 1985, only 37 percent of all mothers received payments from their children's absentee fathers. And the average annual amount of such child support was only $2,220—down by 25 percent in constant dollars from the level of seven years earlier.

Many of these fathers are unemployed and have no money. This means that marriage, or demands for child support, might not improve a young mother's economic condition. To ignore the responsibility that young fathers should have toward their children is to imply that getting girls pregnant is indeed a rite of passage and an expression of power that carries with it no consequences.

Herant Katchadourian, professor of psychiatry and behavioral sciences at Stanford University, bluntly states: "Boys who are sexually active tend to be characterized as 'studs,' while their female counterparts are seen as 'sluts'."

The National Research Council suggests in its report *Risking the Future* that "providing adolescents with employment programs while they are still in school may help to encourage them to avoid early parenthood, especially if the part-time jobs also offer the kind of training that leads to employment after graduation. It cites Maryland's call to government departments "to develop a bold, comprehensive plan of action to alleviate the chronic and worsening high rate of unemployment among high-risk teens."

Lisbeth B. Schorr comments: "When the whole neighborhood is made up of families without fathers or a consistent male presence, not only the income but also the discipline and role models that fathers traditionally have provided are missing. Boys are left to learn about manhood on the streets, where the temptation is strong to demonstrate prowess through law-breaking, violence, and fathering a child."

No effective effort to reduce teenage pregnancies can afford to ignore the way in which society tends to put most of the blame on the girl, without holding the male responsible. The double standard, which at least tacitly makes allowances for sexually irresponsible male behavior, continues to put young women, and their babies, at risk.

BREAKING THE TABOOS: REALISTIC SEX EDUCATION
AND HEALTH CARE

The cycle of unprotected adolescent sex, of babies born to children, of the transmission of disease to pregnant mothers and their infants, must be broken. This cannot be done through preaching or through such slogans as "Just Say No." Diverse and complex issues are involved, from the improvement of the environment in which teenagers live to medical prevention of damage to pregnant women and their babies before and after birth. But at the start, the battle must be waged against ignorance. And to fight ignorance, we must first acknowledge reality.

International statistics indicate clearly that there is little difference in the age at which adolescents in other industrial countries and in the United States become sexually active. Yet, as already shown, the United States leads all others in the number of early adolescent births. For example, even though the Scandinavian countries have long had a reputation for sexual permissiveness, the American incidence of early adolescent pregnancies is seven times that of Sweden's. The lower rate of unwanted births in Sweden is clearly the result of greater knowledge, a willingness to acknowledge the realities of earlier puberty and earlier sexual activity, and a national awareness of the need for timely information about all the possible options in response to the realities—from abstinence to birth control and abortion.

One integral part of a more rational approach is a recognition of the potential of sex education. For generations, sex education has been the butt of jokes and the target of ideological opponents who condemn any forthright discussion of sex in the classroom. These critics charge that teaching about sex encourages sexual experimentation and even promiscuity and that young adolescents' morals are corrupted by a frank discussion of sexuality. Such fears and charges often result in a self-fulfilling prophecy: sex education fails because it does not acknowledge early adolescent sexual activity and frequently is not offered until the high school years.

Researchers agree that merely taking some sex education courses probably does little to change adolescents' sexual behavior. As is true of most academic subjects, sex education is likely to be effective only if it engages young people's thinking and their powers of decision making.

In refreshing counterpoint to the kind of too-cursory, too-dull, or too-delayed sex education that fails to engage or impress adolescents, a three-year study by Girls Incorporated (formerly Girls Clubs of America) seems to point the way to success. Girls Incorporated found that pregnancies among a group of 750 girls between the ages of twelve and seventeen, who were at higher than average risk of becoming pregnant before their high school graduations, were greatly reduced by a cost-effective and candid program that gave them confidence in the present and hope for the future. The program supplied them with communication skills, facts about sexuality, and reproductive health services. The result was that pregnancies among girls ages fifteen to seventeen were reduced by half; only half of the girls between ages twelve and fourteen, who were otherwise at high risk of beginning sexual activity, had sex.

Conducted in Dallas, Memphis, Omaha, and Wilmington, Delaware, the Girls Incorporated program included mother-daughter workshops to remove the taboo from sexual issues and encourage communication. Assertiveness training offered girls models for maintaining friendships without succumbing to peer pressure to engage in sexual activity. Expectations were raised about the prospect of achieving educational and carer goals. Relevant skills were taught as a corrective to reliance on early motherhood for a sense of identity. Girls were given information about sexuality along with access to community-based health services, including contraceptive services. Heather Johnston Nicholson, who directed the project, noted that the full program was supplied at an annual cost of only $116 per girl.

The Girls Incorporated study is particularly valuable because it acknowledges that, without adult help, young people are exposed to narrow and misguided perceptions of the world, including even how their own peers behave. For example, adolescents may believe, and be encouraged to believe, that their friends, though in fact still virgins, are sexually active and therefore more sophisticated than they. While pressure to engage in sexual activity often comes from men and boys, it may also be generated among girls. Virgins are likely to be friends with other virgins, but if one member of the circle becomes sexually active, the others may either break the ties of friendship or follow the "sophisticated" example. In any event, behavior, then, is being shaped not by knowledge but by anxiety and ignorance.

Such ignorance is often reinforced by the role the peer group plays in the development of adolescent values and behavior. This is not to say that adolescent behavior approximates that of *Animal House* movies and other such entertainment that exploits some adults' pruriently distorted views of young people's ways. In fact, many adolescents, particularly girls, are idealistic about sex and love. Perhaps in keeping with society's long-standing double standard, boys tend to look on sex in a more free-wheeling, less committed way. Carol A. Beck, the principal of Thomas Jefferson High School in Brooklyn, puts it plainly: "Girls seek sex for love; boys talk love for sex."

Stanford's Katchadourian observes that in the past, American society addressed adolescent sexuality mainly by trying to suppress or ignore it. Because adults now seem to have lost control over the sexual behavior of adolescents, the attention has shifted to containing the damage. Yet, adults find it difficult to agree on how to go about this task. What values to espouse? What limits to set? All agree that, ideally, the battle against sexual ignorance ought to start in the child's home. Indeed, the conservative view, which so often opposes such initiatives as sex education in school, continues to insist that it is up to parents to teach their children about sex and sexual behavior. Unfortunately, this portrayal of such family-based sex education is often based on myth.

Even in the most stable and healthy families, sex education has been a matter of uneasily shifting responsibilities from one parent to another. Often, too, very different implicit messages are sent out from mother and father to the youngster. Fathers may encourage or, at least, condone their sons' sexual activity, while mothers are opposed to it. Whatever guidance is eventually offered frequently comes after the fact, when the child has already become sexually active. And even if the parents suspect sexual activity, many behave as if failing to acknowledge it means that it does not exist. Often, parents are afraid of widening the generation gap by talking about their own moral principles, which they fear may be outdated.

Unfortunately, the unvarnished reality is that in many American families there is little enlightening communication between parents and children. At best, there may be some expectation that children learn by osmosis—from their parents' example. In fact, the children of well-educated parents with high expectations and certain defined standards of behavior tend not only to be more successful in school but also to be less likely to engage in early, unprotected sexual intercourse. Research also shows that there is a strong relationship between a mother's own sexual experience as a teenager and that of her teenage daughter. Daughters of mothers who show little affection but set strict limits are more likely to engage in early sex. Sexual acting-out may be part of adolescent rebellion; sex becomes a weapon to provoke or humiliate parents. Teenagers who have a close relationship with their parents are more likely to delay their sexual activity—particularly when parents and children agree on values.

LEARNING ABOUT SEXUALITY IN SCHOOL

The report *Turning Points* stressed the importance of reorganizing schools for the middle grade years in ways that would make it possible for every teenager to have one teacher or other adult to whom to turn with personal as well as academic problems. The guiding idea is to create a continuing, close relationship between the young adolescent and a caring, knowledgeable adult acting as confidant and trusted adviser.

All education that deals with human sexuality must begin with moral issues: the sanctity of life; the value of a well-nourished and well-cared-for childhood; the meaning of religious and family values; the benefits of marriage and long-term, stable relationships among mother, father, and children; the impact of sexual activity on one's partner; and the possibility and the consequences of pregnancy—including the advantages of delaying parenthood to a mature age. One of the central developmental tasks of adolescence is to form a sexual identity, and young people must be supported in this often daunting process.

But the humane and intelligent approach to sexual behavior also begins with an understanding of the human body. Katchadourian proposes that the life sciences be creatively employed to tap into the natural curiosity of young adolescents about living organisms in general and their own lives in particular. Teenagers are in the midst of experiencing the unexpected onrush of their growth—one of the most remarkable developmental changes in the entire human life span. They grapple with such questions as What's actually happening to my body? How does a human body work? How do I resemble my friends? How does my stage of physical development differ from theirs?

Starting to teach the life sciences at this point of growth and development seems a valuable and appropriate way to try to answer these questions. The human biology program reverses the traditional sequence of teaching science in general and biology in particular. Instead of beginning with the study of plants and animals, it focuses immediately on human life—the starting point being the young student's own life. Beginning with the phenomenon of puberty, it explores how individuals and society respond to it and soon moves directly to sexuality, the reproductive system, and the ways of guarding and maintaining sexual health.

This leads naturally to the study of behavior. Since high-risk behavior during adolescence bears strongly on health throughout life, there is no better time to capture young people's attention and alert them to the long-term harm done than by a vari-

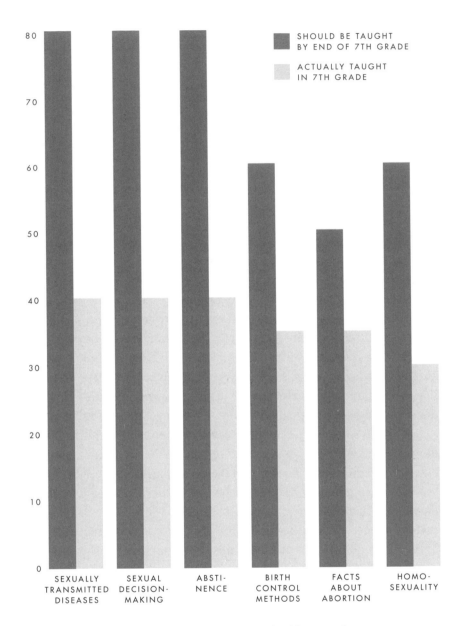

When Teachers Think Sex Education Topics Should Be Taught

PERCENTAGE OF TEACHERS

Source: Alan Guttmacher Institute (1989). *Risk and Responsibility: Teaching Sex Education in America's Schools Today.*

ety of dangerous activities, including early, uninformed, and un-protected sex.

This early focus on life science aims at three goals: engen-dering interest in the study of science in general; making the connection between biology, chemistry, and physics; and pro-moting an understanding of the human body as an important step toward treating it with reason and respect. Integrating the biological and behavioral sciences, the program includes the study of ecology, evolution, and genetics; physiology; human de-velopment (intellectual, psychological, and social); society and culture; and health and safety.

Human biology tries to eliminate past mistakes in introducing young people to matters of sexual behavior, such as the boredom of some traditional sex education taught by teachers who merely follow the manual and stay clear of controversy, or the transmis-sion of information by ignorant, snickering peers. Instead, human biology capitalizes on young teenagers' natural curiosity about the world around them and, in particular, in the changes that are tak-ing place in their own bodies and their emotions. Understanding may not provide ironclad insurance that adolescents will not take unnecessary risks, but it is preferable to ignorance.

Although the human biology program was originally de-signed for undergraduates, Katchadourian and a team of re-searchers are currently adapting it for use in the elementary and middle-school years. If the response at this age level is pos-itive, then the emerging program could become the cornerstone of a rational and persuasive approach to in-school sex education.

ADOLESCENTS AND SEXUAL ACTIVITY IN THE AGE OF AIDS

The threat of AIDS now makes it virtually impossible and en-tirely irresponsible to ignore the necessity of early sex ed-ucation for young people. (At present, fewer than 10 per-cent of all students are exposed to comprehensive sex education.) The threat is real precisely because so many ado-lescents engage in unprotected sex.

By the end of September 1990, more than 147,000 cases of AIDS had been reported in the United States. Given the long incubation period for AIDS—up to ten years—many young adults may suffer from the disease now because they engaged in risky sexual behavior during their adolescent years. There is growing evidence that the incidence of AIDS among adolescents is increasing. While most states now provide AIDS education to adolescents, much of it is of poor quality; some courses, for example, do not even mention intercourse.

In 1989, the Division of Adolescent and School Health of the federal Centers for Disease Control conducted a national survey among students to determine their beliefs, knowledge, and behavior about AIDS in order to evaluate existing education efforts. Students were asked, "Have you been taught about AIDS/HIV (human immunodeficiency virus) infection in school?" Fifty-four percent of all 8,098 students from 122 selected schools said they had received some form of instruction. Based on a questionnaire with seventeen "yes" or "no" items, nearly all students correctly identified the two most frequent ways of transmission of the virus: sharing drug-injecting needles and having sex with an infected partner. Ninety-one percent knew that the virus could be passed on by a pregnant woman to her baby.

But other questions revealed that the students still held beliefs that would put them at serious risk. For example, 12 percent thought that birth control pills provided some protection against the virus, and 23 percent believed that it was possible for them to tell by looking at a potential partner whether she or he was infected.

About 33 percent of students who said they had intercourse reported that they always used condoms; another 17 percent said they sometimes did; 8 percent said they did so only rarely; and 13 percent said they never used condoms. The percentage of those who said they always used condoms declined steadily with advancing age—from 43.5 percent in the ninth grade to 26.4 percent in the twelfth.

What may distort the data regarding the upper grades of high school is that by then many youngsters had dropped out of school, and they were no longer part of the sampling process. This makes it crucial that the message about the risks of AIDS infection be carried beyond the schools to youth groups, clinics, and such public places as the shopping malls where adolescents tend to hang out. The *Journal of Adolescent Health Care* notes that peer counseling, which makes it easier for some adolescents to ask sex-related questions, may be particularly useful in such settings.

Many adults act as irresponsible models for young people by behaving as if dangerous attitudes or conditions will simply disappear if they are unacknowledged. Research conducted in Australia and reported in the *Journal of Adolescent Research* (April 1991) suggests that teenagers tend to believe that they are unique and invulnerable to "risks and hazards which beset other mortals." Young people often harbor the illusion that although others may suffer the consequences of dangerous actions, they are somehow immune. In 1987, a report by the World Health Organization's Global Programme on AIDS urged that such misconceptions be taken into account in any planning and targeting of AIDS intervention strategies.

An earlier start of sexual activity, of course, exposes young adolescents not only to the risk of AIDS but also to other sexually transmitted diseases. The United States is experiencing an alarming rise in syphilis. Sexually active girls between the ages of ten and nineteen had the highest rate of gonorrhea of any age group. Similar data about syphilis and chlamydia also show the highest rates among adolescents — not, as is generally believed, among adults. It is a fair guess that adolescents who contract other sexually transmitted diseases also expose themselves to the risk of AIDS, and this means that, as the incidence of AIDS and HIV infection increases, the number of infected adolescents will rise rapidly.

Ignorance greatly heightens the risk. The *Journal of Adolescent Research* (January 1990) concludes: "Unfortunately, adolescents have not changed sexual practices nor methods of contraception as a result of the AIDS epidemic." The *Journal* editors regard school- and community-based prevention programs as urgently needed.

A report in the *American Journal of Public Health* (March 1990) showed that adolescents who engaged in intercourse after drinking or smoking marijuana were respectively 2.8 and 1.9 times less likely to use condoms.

Attitudes that make adults uneasy about using contraceptives are even more pronounced among adolescents. For example, in general, both boys and girls tend to feel awkward about the use of contraceptive devices, especially condoms, during their first sexual encounter or, subsequently, in an encounter with a new partner. Intercourse often has not been planned, and being prepared for it may offend the partner and suggest promiscuity. Girls, and to a lesser degree boys, are often embarrassed to ask the new partner about his or her previous sexual encounters. In moments of passion (or lust), such inquiries, if they enter the couples' minds at all, may sound like a betrayal of trust. Romantic emotions easily get in the way of sexual *realpolitik*, and the question of whether contraception is a male or female responsibility has not been answered to the satisfaction of many sexually active youngsters.

All of the above illustrates the gap between changing sexual behavior and a rational answer to its dangers. While these uncertainties underscore the importance of trying to persuade more young people to postpone sexual activity, they also illuminate the need to deal with the issues earlier and more explicitly than once was considered proper, or even useful. The stakes are too high not to address the risks openly and not to eliminate the old taboos.

The Robert Wood Johnson Foundation has underwritten a special program to train peer counselors as popular advisers on sex education. It reports: "Program training was designed to be self-affirming and empowering. By creating and acting out social dilemmas in role plays, students have developed their behavioral strategies and social skills. By discussing the issues in focus groups, worldview explorations, and film and music analyses, they have exercised their critical thinking skills and legitimated their opinions. By creating and developing their own videos, public service announcements, and assorted educational materials, they have gained a sense of control. . . . By practicing with cucumbers, they have overcome embarrassment and have gained the specific knowledge and skills to describe and/or demonstrate the proper use of condoms. By conducting their own school-wide educational efforts, they have gained recognition from their peers as experts."

The Alan Guttmacher Institute reports that, although AIDS/HIV education is increasing in schools, it still is not offered to all students in all secondary schools. Yet, there has been progress: in 1988, seventeen states required such instruction, and in 1989 twenty-eight did so. However, some of the instruction remains superficial.

The National Research Council cites condom distribution programs aimed especially at young men "as a potentially promising means of encouraging male involvement in pregnancy prevention." Yet, contraceptive advertising frequently runs into public opposition or even outright prohibition. Recently, Wisconsin enacted legislation to remove restrictions against such advertising, and South Carolina and Delaware recommend such advertising as part of a statewide media campaign. The South Carolina campaign would promote "the responsible use of contraception by those teenagers who are sexually active." This fits into growing efforts to teach young men that family planning is not a female issue. One proposal in Maine points out that "most boys do not know how to use contraceptives properly and do not know whom to ask for information." The District of Columbia has recommended a media campaign on the theme "Don't make a baby if you can't be a father."

Young people need to perceive that raising a family can be exciting and satisfying when they are mature enough to understand its responsibilities, as well as its joys. In some ways, positive family life education may appear to be a cruel enterprise. Depicting the way a family "ought" to behave might be humiliating, even shocking, to youngsters whose own experience is tragically different—lacking in nurture and deprived of human warmth. Is it fair, for example, to describe the caring and supportive role a father can play to a teenager who is growing up in a fatherless household? Or to talk about responsible and joyful sex to an adolescent who may have seen his own family members subjected to exploitative or even violent sexual activity?

And yet, young people must be given an opportunity to understand what family life can be like and the hope that they can make it so for themselves. When family planning is explored as part of the adolescents' capacity to make personal decisions about their own future family life, questions of how to prevent unplanned pregnancies, unwanted children, and sexual intercourse with untrustworthy partners will not appear so controversial.

It must also be acknowledged, however, that children who grow up in two-parent families may not be immune to serious problems. On the other hand, children of one-parent families may achieve stable and successful lives. Many do just that. But having only one parent can be a serious disadvantage. For example, the National Association of Elementary School Principals found that 30 percent of the pupils who came from two-parent families turned out to be high achievers, compared to only 17 percent from single-parent homes.

A 1990 Census Bureau survey shows that almost 25 percent of all American children of the 1980s and 1990s, and 60 percent of all black children under the age of eighteen, are living with a single parent. Of the children in single-parent households, 38.6 percent are living with a divorced parent, and 30.6 percent are living with a parent who has never married.

Ever since the growth of the one-parent family, there has been a tendency to accept it as virtually normal. Too many social commentators portray the birth of children out of wedlock as part of "the norm." What actually amounts to abandoning children, usually by the father, is becoming increasingly acceptable without penalty to anyone except to the neglected child.

Too many social scientists and policymakers play down the advantages of the two-parent family; some even ridicule it as an outmoded middle-class ideal.

Such views have the effect of condoning young males' and boys' sexual irresponsibility, and this clashes head-on with the interest of women and children. Decrying the decline of the traditional family should not be considered square or old-fashioned.

GETTING HEALTH CARE

As long as teenagers become mothers, intentionally or not, it is crucial for them to have access to prenatal care. At present, many of their babies are brought into the world with dangerously low birthweight and serious physical and mental handicaps that could have been prevented if the pregnant girls had been given proper attention.

For more than a decade, from the 1960s to 1979, the percentage of all women getting sound prenatal care rose steadily, partly as a result of Medicaid and private insurance support. But in the 1980s, that proportion began dropping among black women and teenagers of all races. Cutbacks in government support affected these women and girls at high risk. As a result, in 1983 the proportion of low-birthweight babies rose in twenty-one states. The period also marked the first time in eighteen years that the proportion of low-birthweight babies rose among white infants.

Over the years, black and Hispanic women, poor and poorly educated women, and very young girls have been least likely to get prenatal care in time, or at all. Yet, these potential mothers are at the greatest risk of producing damaged or unhealthy babies who will continue to be a drain on their mothers' energies and earning power.

Major causes of this critical situation are the women's lack of access to money and insurance coverage. Reimbursement policies for Medicaid fluctuate from state to state. Between 1980 and 1985, at least seventy public hospitals were closed for financial reasons. Growing pressures to contain medical costs deny care to large numbers of people who cannot afford to pay and who are uninsured. At the same time, economic incentives drive physicians toward administering intensive care and high technology treatment of disease, rather than propelling them toward desperately needed preventive care.

Arnold Relman, speaking of the problem for the Institute of Medicine, commented: "The method by which most physicians are paid now seems, on a number of grounds, to be rather a poor reflection of society's objectives for health care.... It provides large rewards for the provision of high-technology procedures and little or none for preventive and cognitive activities." Yet, it is precisely that kind of activity that would improve prenatal care for pregnant teenagers.

Certain factors are not dollar related. For example, despite all the evidence that smoking endangers the growth of the fetus, obstetricians do not emphasize enough the danger to pregnant women they treat. Alcohol consumption and any drug use during pregnancy could cause babies to be born with damaged central nervous systems and serious malformations. Yet, the medical profession as a whole takes too little responsibility for helping expectant mothers to abstain from drugs and alcohol, and many practitioners even fail to mention these facts to their patients—partly because their questions are not geared to eliciting such information as, for example, the use of wine coolers that contain alcohol or diet pills that contain harmful amphetamines.

Proper counseling and treatment are often neglected because they are time consuming. Lisbeth Schorr, in citing constructive examples, quotes Jenie James, a nurse-midwife in South Carolina, about her care for pregnant teenagers: "We take a great deal of time with each girl. We feel it is important not to generalize about anything, but to find out about her ... to ask about social and emotional issues and to take time for behavioral problems and questions." And Sarah Piechnick, another nurse-midwife, said: "It can take an hour to establish rapport.

If you're rushed, there's no communication. It takes time to enlist people—especially adolescents and very poor women—in their own care, and allow the discovery process to unfold."

Pregnant teenagers often present special problems. Because they want to prevent the pregnancy from "ruining" their appearance, or because they want to hide the fact that they are pregnant, they may continue to wear jeans that are too tight or diet to keep their weight down, thereby stunting the growth of the fetus.

Ultimately, much depends on effective, large-scale programs and state and/or national policies. One example of what could be achieved is a California program called Access to Obstetrical Care (OB Access Project). In addition to supplying medical services starting early in pregnancy, including a complete screening for medical risks, it provides women with a thorough nutritional assessment, vitamin supplements, a psychological evaluation and follow-up services, health education, coordination with the Special Supplemental Food Program for Women, Infants and Children, family planning services, and parenting classes. If a woman is unable to attend classes because of a health, language, cultural, job, or transportation problem, she can obtain individual instruction. An outreach and media-supported program aims at women in need of special prenatal attention. Eventually, almost 7,000 women were registered, 25 percent of them teenagers. Fifty percent were Mexican-Americans, 25 percent were white, and 10 percent were black.

The results justify the effort. The percentage of low-birthweight babies was a third lower among these women than a comparable group who were not in the program. The percentage of very low birthweight was less than half that of the comparison group. The program's initial costs were more than recouped by the relatively low expenditures needed for intensive care after birth.

In another experiment in Baltimore, Johns Hopkins University Hospital provided "prenatal-plus" services in a bright storefront clinic at a slightly seedy shopping center. All participants were seventeen-year-olds or younger, most of them black, single, and poor. Janet Hardy, the program's founder, said: "Pregnant adolescents need more than good medical care. They need more services, a case management system to assure that no problem is overlooked, and—perhaps most important of all—they need an environment which makes them feel comfortable and cared about."

The Johns Hopkins team dealing with pregnant teenagers consists of an obstetrician, two obstetrical nurses, a social worker, and a health educator. In addition to medical and health problems, the team makes it its business to address the girls' schoolwork and job prospects; their fears about childbirth and/or motherhood; their relationships with family and friends; and their worries about where they will live and how they will take care of the baby. "Waiting until after delivery to talk about the job of being a parent is too late," Hardy said.

One problem in replicating the program in the wake of its undeniable success is that, in order to work, it must remain small. "Huge doesn't work," one of the team members said.

In a broad sense, the best way to protect adolescents' health may be through the facilities where most of these young people are: in the schools. There can be little doubt that well-organized and expertly staffed school-based or, at the very least, school-related, health centers can lead to a large-scale improvement in adolescent health. Regrettably, this approach often collides head-on with active foes of birth control and family planning. Nevertheless, the care of adolescent health and the prevention of health-threatening behavior address the totality of young people's physical, mental, and emotional well-being, and contraceptive counseling and family planning ought to be an integral part of such centers' responsibilities. There is no indication that students' sexual activity increases or decreases when such services become available, but a survey of students in a school that is part of Houston's school-based health center showed that those who made use of the center were more than twice as likely to use contraception every time they had intercourse as their peers who had not visited the center. (See chapter 2.)

In parallel findings, a Kansas City survey also showed that boys who used the center's services reported a striking increase in the use of condoms. In St. Paul, Minnesota, one effect of the center was the very high rate of girls who continued to use contraceptives (mostly the birth control pill)—91 percent after a year—while centers not related to schools found that almost 50 percent stopped using contraception within twelve months.

Still, even these favorable reports offer no conclusive evidence that all of these factors significantly reduce pregnancy or birth rates. Researchers also point out that students represent a highly mobile population and that the number of abortions, for example, remains seriously underreported.

As noted earlier, to assure the success of school-related centers, it is essential to concentrate on the training of participating health providers—physicians, nurses, and counselors—so that they understand adolescents and their development and are comfortable with them.

Whatever the specific location, in or near school, health facilities must be physically placed so that young adolescents, in middle or junior high schools, and even in upper elementary grades, know that such help is within reach of their school and that it is "user friendly." The services must also reach out to those young people who are not attending school.

Most reports share a common belief: that sensible, responsible, and normal adolescent behavior is the product of a combination of forces—educational and economic—that build self-confidence and pride. An Illinois report puts it simply: "Students should be helped to see that they can control their destinies and give meaning to their lives." But controlling destiny and finding meaning in life is difficult for youngsters who live in dismal surroundings where they constantly see adults who have lost control over their own destinies and who no longer find meaning in their lives. These teenagers need much support—by churches and synagogues, community groups, and, on a daily basis, in schools—to help them break out of the cycle of hopelessness and to acquire the skills and the confidence to take control over their lives and their emotions.

None of the programs cited can guarantee that young teenagers will avoid early pregnancy, unwanted childbirth, and premature parenthood, but they offer the best hope that young people will learn to make decisions and to consider the consequences of their actions based on a better understanding of their body, mind, and emotions. To that end, they need the support of adults who are aware of the problems and aspirations of adolescents and who will not approach them with intimidation or antagonism.

Jane Quinn of Carnegie Corporation's Council on Adolescent Development, who was formerly a program manager at Girls Incorporated, noted that by ages twelve to fourteen, 25 percent of the participants of the organization's study described earlier had engaged in sexual intercourse: "Preventing teenage pregnancies requires much more than a 'Just say no' approach . . . the lessons have to start early, preferably by age nine."

The poignant and immensely promising results of that study alone should convince us that providing confidence, pride, life skills, and early access to family planning information and services is, today, an indispensable prerequisite for the health of all adolescents.

CHAPTER FOUR

DRUGS, ALCOHOL, CIGARETTES

n 1948, when a leading college introduced a new curriculum, one of its planners, asked what the reform was intended to accomplish, said: "To teach students to consider the consequences of their actions."

At the time, this concept hardly seemed revolutionary, especially when it referred to carefully selected college students. Today, the consideration of consequences has reemerged in a different context: drug and alcohol abuse by teenagers. As Joy G. Dryfoos observes: "In this field, young people who do not believe in the consequences of their actions are more likely to be heavy users."

The judgment, of course, applies to every kind of at-risk behavior but particularly to cigarette smoking, driving under the influence of alcohol and drugs, and engaging in unprotected sexual activity. The consequences of such behavior can be profound indeed. It follows that teaching young people to consider the consequences of their actions is at the heart of any effective educational approach to drug, alcohol, and smoking prevention.

In case there is any doubt about the serious consequences of these activities, a few facts should allay them. The U.S. Department of Health and Human Services, in its 1990 report *Healthy People 2000* points out that tobacco use is responsible for more than one in every six deaths in the United States. It is the most important single preventable underlying cause of death and disease and accounts for about 390,000 deaths a year, including 21 percent of all deaths attributed to coronary heart disease, 30 percent of all deaths attributed to cancer generally (or all cancers), and 87 percent of all deaths attributed to lung cancer. Smoking during pregnancy accounts for 20 to 30 percent of all low-birthweight babies, up to 14 percent of preterm deliveries, and 10 percent of infant deaths. Anyone who still is not convinced of the importance of preventing smoking should be alerted to the fact that youngsters hooked on tobacco at an early age were found to have other serious problems as well. They were more likely to do poorly in school, engage in disruptive and otherwise troublesome behavior, and have difficult relations within their families.

Alcohol problems are estimated to cost the nation more than $70 billion a year. Alcohol is the cause of nearly half of the deaths caused by motor vehicle accidents, suicides, and homicides. Forty-four billion dollars in national economic costs are attributed to the use of illegal drugs.

Since alcohol, cigarettes, and drugs are addictive or at the very least habit forming, how early adolescents regard them is not only of immediate concern but is the most serious problem for the long term.

Effective prevention has proved difficult. If it is to have any chance for success, one must first consider why young people turn to drugs. To some extent, using drugs is a form of self-medication for depression and other distress. However dangerous and misguided, it is an effort at coping. In the difficult state of trying to leave childhood behind and appear grown up, many teenagers use drugs as a way of feeling strong, brave, competent, and sophisticated. Considering how many adults turn to drugs in search of power and status, it is condescending not to take seriously the adolescents' far more understandable feelings of insecurity. The adults' task is to help adolescents find the security they seek through ways that are both practical and less dangerous and to aid teenagers in the transition toward young adulthood without jeopardizing their health and their futures.

Unfortunately, most of the commercial and cultural messages aimed at young people stress the lures of instant pleasure, ignoring the consequences of unhealthy or dangerous actions. Alcohol advertisements associate their products with good fellowship and fun, including the camaraderie of sports, and with achieving confidence and success with the opposite sex. So does cigarette advertising. The joys of glamorized, impromptu, unprotected sex are the staple of movies, television, and rock music, and they are convincing indeed. As noted earlier, a recent report in the *American Journal of Public Health* (March 1990) showed that adolescents who engaged in intercourse after drinking or smoking marijuana were respectively 2.8 and 1.9 times less likely to use condoms. The occasional public service message warning against these risks cannot begin to compete with the continuous appeal to ignore the consequences.

Society's own message about both the immediate and the long-term dangers of drugs has also often been confusing. During the 1960s and early 1970s, many adults, wanting to be on the youth side of the generation gap, publicly played down the harmful effect of drugs, or even urged their acceptance. Unfortunately, such opinions were widely expressed by certain university faculty members, psychologists, and others who had reputations as experts or otherwise commanded the respect of young people; they contradicted those who warned about drugs' potential dangers and sometimes even pressed the matter of drug use as a civil liberties issue. Marijuana was regularly defended as neither harmful nor addictive, and the benign image was frequently extended to harder substances, including those associated with hallucinations.

Such misguided voices have largely fallen silent, but their effect lingers. In recent years, the appeal of drugs has been rekindled by its glorification in pop music and by certain rock stars and even athletes, who are quite naturally viewed by many adolescents as role models. The fact that an addicted young adolescent lacks the enormous resources that are brought to bear in rehabilitating a revered and addicted music or sports hero is just one sad paradox in the tragic romance of the drug culture.

The abuse of harmful, even deadly, substances is neither new nor confined to the United States, and the fact that so many countries have argued about the pros and cons of legalizing drugs offers testimony of their universal prevalence. Much publicity has been given to recent efforts in Russia to reduce the consumption of alcohol because of its disastrous impact not only on public health and safety but on the industrial productivity of the nation. The Scandinavian countries have long attempted to reduce their peoples' excessive drinking, and no Swedish organization would accept financial support from an alcohol producer in exchange for the company's good will.

In the United States, the demand for illegal, addictive drugs is backed by vast sums of money. Even at the lowest level, in the streets of poor neighborhoods, the lure of thousands of dollars to be made in drug sales by entrepreneurial youngsters who otherwise could barely expect minimum wages—if they could find jobs at all—is immense. This hopelessness about a future devoid of legal economic security is what propels so many young people to engage in the alternative violent culture of drug sales. In 1989, the number of murders in Washington, D.C., averaged more than one a day, and more than 70 percent were related to drugs.

It is a widespread misconception that drug problems are confined to the poor, largely because the results of drug use— homelessness, street crime, and violence—are most visible in poor communities, on the streets, and in the headlines and on television. The fact is that drug abuse is far more common than is generally recognized among the middle class and affluent sectors; the difference is that this population has the capacity to hide the problem and its consequences from public view and to afford private treatment and rehabilitation.

THE DIMENSIONS OF THE PROBLEM

That most drug use is confined to the poor is only one popular myth about drugs. There is also a widespread misconception that drugs affect mainly black youths. In fact, the most recent annual study conducted for the federal government by the University of Michigan's Institute for Social Research showed that black high school seniors are less likely to use drugs than their white classmates. The study, based on responses from 73,000 high school seniors and considered the most comprehensive survey to date of teenage drug use, showed that more than 40 percent of white boys said they had smoked marijuana during the one-year period, compared to 29.8 percent of blacks; only 18.4 percent of black girls said that they had smoked marijuana, compared to 36 percent of whites. Nearly 12 percent of the white boys said that they had tried cocaine during the one-year period, compared to 6.1 percent of blacks. For white and black girls, the figures were 9.3 percent and 2.6 percent, respectively. The figures may require some readjustment because more black youngsters drop out of school before high school graduation and therefore are not included in the percentages.

Nevertheless, there are compelling reasons why young black adolescents may turn away from using drugs. Commenting on the research findings, Kevin Zeese, vice president for the Drug Policy Foundation, said: "Black communities are faced with open drug dealing in their streets; they see the crime and the horror associated with drugs." He emphasized the need to correct the image that drugs are only a black problem.

In reality, then, drug use is a national scourge from which no segment of our population is immune. And while drug addiction also spares no age group, attention should focus on addiction's impact on youth for two reasons: youthful addiction produces serious long-term consequences, and young adolescents are at special risk because they naturally like to experiment and explore. Many find it difficult to resist the challenge by their peers to "try" illegal drugs, alcohol, and cigarettes.

The extent of substance abuse among adolescents is alarming. For many, drinking becomes excessive and dangerous at an early age to the point of endangering their health and their success in school and their personal lives. A survey by the National Institute on Drug Abuse reported that one in twenty students among the high school class of 1987 had used alcohol daily during the month before the survey. In addition, and even more troubling, 37 percent of the seniors (46 percent of the boys and 29 percent of the girls) had taken five or more drinks in a single session during the prior two weeks, 19 percent had smoked cigarettes daily, and 3 percent had used marijuana daily.

In a 1991 update, U.S. Surgeon General Antonia Novello noted that, of the nation's 20.7 million students in seventh through twelfth grade, 8 million drink alcohol weekly, and 454,000 have five or more consecutive drinks at least once a week. Many of those who go on such weekly sprees, Novello said, "are already alcoholics, and the rest may be on the way."

Contrary to another popular misconception, boys do not greatly outnumber girls in regard to problem drinking. Of those who engage in binge drinking, or five or more drinks in a row, 59 percent are male and 41 percent female. The average "binger" is sixteen years old and was twelve years old when he or she took the first drink. The *New York Times* (June 23, 1991) reported that a thirteen-year-old girl, the daughter of two lawyers, had been drinking for about four years. She showed up for gymnastics practice at her private school in Massachusetts too drunk to perform.

A fifteen-year-old boy told a juvenile court judge that he was not a "problem drinker" just because he drank a six-pack of beer every night.

"By twelve, most kids know someone who drinks, and they probably know a significant number who drink," says Lloyd Johnston, a social science researcher at the University of Michigan who annually surveys the drinking habits of high school students and has extended his study downward to eighth-graders.

Margaret Bean-Bayog, a psychiatrist in Newton, Massachusetts, observes: "The age of first alcohol use in the 1930s was seventeen for boys and nineteen for women. It has drifted steadily down. Now it's much more common for a thirteen-year-old to have had a drink." Bean-Bayog and other experts urge parents to be aware of the signs of children's drinking: to watch out for changes in a child's behavior, secretiveness, declining grades in school, and giving up old friends in favor of a faster, often hard-drinking, crowd.

As noted in regard to drug use, many students use alcohol as a tool to help them cope with troubled feelings and tense situations. Of the 10.6 million students who drink, 31 percent report that they drink alone, and 41 percent say that they drink when they are upset about something. Twenty-five percent say that they drink because they are bored. Not atypical, an article in a student newspaper observed that beer was popular because it "makes even the most shy people witty and clever at parties." Some students expressed concern over the fact that drinking is the most popular weekend activity. One said he was disappointed that "several of my friends can't be social unless they are drunk (or so they say)."

Such explanations of why they drink differ little from the reasons given by adults for their drinking; the greater risk in the case of teenagers, however, is that an early start often leads to more serious alcohol abuse as time passes.

Francis A. J. Ianni writes in *The Search for Structure: A Report on American Youth Today*: "Our society has, I believe, made the adolescent peer group the scapegoat for some of our own sins, both those we commit ourselves and those sins teenagers learn from us. The use and abuse of drugs, alcohol, and tobacco were all adult problems first and became teenage problems only after we introduced youngsters to them as indicators of an adult life style."

The problem is greatly aggravated by ignorance: adolescents often do not know how much alcohol is contained in what they are drinking, and the alcoholic beverage industry does little to clarify the matter. The Office of Inspector General of the

U.S. Department of Health and Human Services documents the problem in a report, *Youth and Alcohol: Do They Know What They're Drinking?* (June 1991). The study found that two out of three students in junior and senior high school cannot distinguish between alcoholic and nonalcoholic beverages and that industry labeling supports the confusion. In addition, there is much confusion about the alcohol content of products that physically resemble one another. For example, beers generally contain alcohol in proportions of 4.0 to 4.8 percent; but malt liquor, packaged much like beer, contains about twice as much alcohol.

In 1981, the industry introduced "wine coolers," which range from 1.5 to 6 percent alcohol by volume. Junior and senior high school students drink 35 percent of all the wine coolers sold in the United States and 1.1 billion cans of beer each year.

The financial success of wine coolers prompted the industry to introduce mixed drink coolers, which contain 4 percent alcohol. All of these products are easily confused with fortified wines, such as Cisco, Thunderbird, and Night Train, whose 20 percent alcohol content is nearly double that of most table wines and four to five times that of ordinary wine coolers. All are marketed with a variety of fruit flavors, and the bottles are so similar that one is easily mistaken for the other. As a result, students were found to confuse even fruit-flavored mineral waters with a variety of alcoholic drinks.

This confusion was particularly evident in young adolescents. Seventy-three percent of those fifteen or younger did not know that at least one of the alcoholic beverages described contained alcohol. Almost 80 percent of all the students interviewed did not know that "a shot" of liquor contains the same amount of alcohol as a can of beer. About 55 percent did not know that a glass of wine and a can of beer have similar alcohol content. Thirty-six percent did not know that Cisco, with one of the highest alcohol levels (20 percent), is an alcoholic drink at all. A new warning on Cisco bottles, "This is not a wine cooler," only adds to the confusion. One student expressed precisely the response that the manufacturer seemed to be encouraging by noting that he thought it meant that it did not contain alcohol.

The report concluded that the students' own comments emphasize both the dangers and the popularity of such products as Cisco. One student said: "One girl tasted it, said it tasted like Kool-Aid, and drank it fast." Another: "I know a lot of people that blacked out."

The surgeon general calls for coordinated efforts to assure that (1) total alcohol content of all beverages, including beer and malt liquor, be displayed clearly and understandably, and (2) that alcoholic and nonalcoholic beverages be packaged in clearly distinguishable fashion. (This recommendation may make it necessary to repeal an obsolete federal law that prohibits the disclosure of alcohol content on beer containers.) In addition, the *Youth and Alcohol* report urges the surgeon general to consult with public and private agencies to develop, improve, and promote education programs to increase students' knowledge of alcoholic beverages and their effect.

Even though the sale of alcoholic beverages to youths below age twenty-one is prohibited, another report by the Office of Inspector General, *Youth and Alcohol: Drinking Habits, Access, Attitudes, and Knowledge* (June 1991), found that it is often easy for underage young people to obtain alcohol, either directly or with the help of adults. Teenagers as young as twelve or thirteen report that they have no trouble buying alcoholic beverages in a store. Many youngsters use fake identity papers. Almost three-fourths of the seventh-graders who drink get alcohol from their parents. The study found that 1.6 million youngsters do not know that a law exists that prohibits them from buying alcoholic beverages. A substantial proportion of those who do know that such a law exists do not know that the legal drinking age in all states is now twenty-one. (Guesses ranged from fourteen to twenty-four.)

When students were asked about the intoxicating effects of alcohol, more than 2.6 million did not know that an overdose can kill. More than one-third hold the mistaken belief, shared by many adults, that drinking coffee, getting some fresh air, or taking a cold shower will "sober you up." Many believe that they cannot get drunk on wine coolers.

Substance use—of alcohol, illegal drugs, and cigarettes—frequently begins in early adolescence. For example, three out of five high school seniors who have ever used alcohol, and about half of those who have ever used marijuana, first used it before tenth grade. Daily cigarette smoking also begins before tenth grade, or at age fifteen or sixteen, for more than half of those who practice it by the time they are seniors. Similar statistics apply to nearly all other drugs, except for cocaine, which was rarely used before high school according to the class of 1987, though its use in early adolescence has since increased, probably as a result of the availability and low cost of crack cocaine.

As already noted, alcohol is frequently the cause of motor vehicle accidents. In about half of all motor vehicle fatalities involving an adolescent driver, excessive drinking is considered responsible. The situation affects not only those adolescents who are old enough to drive; 32 percent of eighth-graders reported having been passengers in cars driven by an adolescent under the influence of alcohol during the month before they replied to a federal survey. Alcohol is also frequently implicated when adolescents die as pedestrians, or die as a result of using recreational vehicles. Even though 92 percent of all students surveyed by the Office of Inspector General said no person who has been drinking should ever drive, almost one-third said they have accepted rides from drivers who have been drinking.

While adolescent drug use is reported to have declined slightly in recent years, alcohol has become a more serious problem among ten- to fifteen-year-olds over the past two decades. Drinking patterns have changed remarkably. A greater proportion of young adolescents use alcohol, have their first drinking experience earlier, and report more frequent intoxication. Although girls still drink with less frequency than boys, the proportion who drink and who report having been intoxicated has increased more rapidly for girls than for boys. This is also true in regard to cigarette smoking. The gender gap in the use of illegal drugs also has narrowed in the past ten years; regrettably, girls are catching up with the boys' dangerous habits.

School people are particularly concerned about alcohol abuse, not only because of its increase but because it is linked to a variety of disruptive, and often dangerous, behaviors. Joy G. Dryfoos reports that a study of New York State students found that such in-school conduct as cutting classes, being sent to the principal for disciplinary reasons, and low academic achievement are the most important indicators of alcohol consumption. Among students with ten or more reported incidents of misconduct, 93 percent were alcohol drinkers. Among students with failing grades, 82 percent were drinkers. The correlation between alcohol and drug use as well as unprotected sex was also found to be very strong.

The liquor industry, perhaps fearful that it may eventually join the cigarette manufacturers as a prime target of public hostility, has embraced the drive to appoint a "designated driver," someone who is to refrain from drinking among groups of partying friends. Clearly, any arrangement that keeps impaired persons from the steering wheel deserves support; but while the practice may prevent accidents and fatalities, it provides no solution to the problem of excessive drinking in general. As the *Wall Street Journal* (May 21, 1991) put it: "The lobbying [for moderation] is part of a billion-dollar counterattack by the liquor industry against the greatest peril to its business since Prohibition: a binge of anti-drinking criticism by health advocates, parents' groups and others that threatens to do to booze what others have done to cigarettes." The article quotes one industry spokesman: "Either you take the high ground, or you're going down Tobacco Road."

There has been some self-policing by the liquor industry. Hard-liquor companies voluntarily refrain from advertising on television and radio. But there is no such constraint in regard to beer: many of its advertisements target young people, often in connection with drinking after a day at sports. A recent poster advertising malt liquor proclaimed: "It works every time." The ad displayed a beautiful young woman in a pose that left little doubt about just how the drink is supposed to work.

The *Wall Street Journal*, which has been critical of such advertising, recently reported that the U.S. Bureau of Alcohol, Tobacco and Firearms, after long ignoring the matter, has begun to crack down on such appeals. But in general, alcohol advertising, like that for cigarettes, often is aimed directly at teenagers and also at young blacks. Peter Rogers, a Youngstown, Ohio, pediatrician who directs the Child-Adolescent Committee of the American Society of Addictive Medicine, reports that a teenager watching an average amount of television is likely to see 2,500 beer and wine advertisements a year.

The report by the U.S. Department of Health and Human Services notes that liquor advertisements "spotlight attractive people and make drinking look like fun. Some students' comments: "Some of them are funny, and some have sexy women." "They make you look like you're cool and accepted." Or a girl's response: "Girls in the advertisements are skinny, and I want to be like that."

Cigarette advertising also is often aimed at youth and particularly young women, telling them, for example, that they have come a long way by attaining the freedom to smoke in public. This pitch is of particular concern, since young women are currently the only population group that has resisted the antismoking trend. The situation clearly calls for pinpointed campaigns aimed at adolescent girls to urge them not to smoke. Such appeals should be based on factual information that underscores the potential damage not only to themselves but to their future capacity to bear healthy babies. Positive benefits should be stressed: the prevention of health-damaging behavior should rely not so much on prohibition as on the promise of new strengths and lasting satisfaction, as well as immediate benefits, such as success in sports, pleasant breath, and white teeth.

Efforts to reduce girls' cigarette smoking are likely to fail unless attention is paid to the reasons why so many young girls smoke. One major cause is preoccupation with being slim. Since girls have learned that giving up the cigarette addiction often leads to weight gain, they assume that smoking itself avoids putting on unwanted pounds. For many young teenage girls, the immediate threat of not conforming to the much-publicized American ideal of the slim figure outweighs the relatively distant risk of grave dangers to future health. (See chapter 6.)

If adolescents smoke and drink to feel more secure, then what can be done to give them a greater sense of serenity without the need for the crutches of nicotine, alcohol, and drugs? The answers are likely to be the same as those that deter young women from early pregnancies: fostering pride, confidence, and genuine hope for the future.

A September 1991 study by the Office on Smoking and Health at the federal Centers for Disease Control in Atlanta shows that two and a half times as many white high school students as their black classmates smoke and that the rate of smoking among black adolescents has dropped significantly in the past decade. Experts at the Centers attribute the trend in large part to the rise in the cost of a pack of cigarettes from about $.60 in 1980 to $2.00 in 1990. During that period, smoking among white youngsters dropped only slightly, a rare instance of affluence representing a greater threat to health than poverty.

The same study, part of a Youth Risk Behavior Survey, also found that 12.8 percent of the students surveyed were frequent cigarette smokers; about 13 percent of both sexes smoked frequently; and 19 percent of the boys reported using smokeless tobacco, compared to only 1 percent of the girls. By race, 41.2 percent of whites reported tobacco use, compared to 16.8 percent of black teenagers and 32 percent of Hispanics.

The most recent cigarette advertisement that has proven successful in its appeal to teenagers is the creation of a cartoon figure named Old Joe Camel, billed as a "smooth character." Although R. J. Reynolds, the cigarette manufacturer, insists that the ads are aimed at adults, a series of studies, published in the December 1991 issue of the *Journal of the American Medical*

Association, show a substantial increase in Camel's share of the illegal cigarette market aimed at children. Promotions and give-aways, based on purchase of Camel packages, include Old Joe T-shirts, Camel baseball caps, Camel watches, and "a Camel-em-blazoned inflatable mattress with a radio."

Probably as a result of the misguided adult views noted ear-lier, which were accorded a great deal of publicity at the time, a striking increase in marijuana use began in the second half of the 1960s. It has leveled off in recent years, perhaps because of a change in adult attitudes. In sharp contrast to previous claims, it has been found that early use of marijuana often leads to the use of more dangerous drugs. But, even in the short-term, it in-terferes with performance and safety. Still, more than half of all high school seniors have had some experience with marijuana, and, after a brief decline, its use increased again after 1985, par-ticularly among school dropouts.

Drugs that are illegally manufactured and sold account for a great number of medical emergencies, partly because they are often contaminated or of variable and unpredictable potency. The use of two or more such drugs, when combined with alco-hol, greatly increases the risk to health and even to life. Cocaine, though long known as an addictive drug, has come to be recog-nized as a major public health threat only in recent years. As its use has increased, particularly in the form of crack, so has the appearance of its victims in emergency rooms. In addition to causing deaths by overdose, crack has created immense medi-cal and social problems.

PREVENTING SUBSTANCE ABUSE: WHAT WORKS?

Although some methods of treatment interrupt and even terminate addictions, the long-term results are at best spotty and subject to failure unless constructive pressure is maintained long enough and the original motivation for the substance abuse is eliminated or at least lessened. Effective follow-through tends to be most difficult in an environment of poverty and lawlessness. As in the case of early pregnancies, there frequently is a close connection between young people's drift into drug use and school failure that results in a decline in self-esteem and closed options for success after school.

Current research into what preventive measures are effective and desirable once again reflects society's own ambivalence about what values to impart to the next generation. For example, in response to a request by Senator John Glenn, the U.S. General Accounting Office (GAO), a research arm of Congress, has issued a report, *Drug Education: School-based Programs Seen as Useful but Impact Unknown.* Addressing alcohol, the GAO reported a split among experts: on one side, it found school districts whose representatives insisted that alcohol use is wrong and harmful and that the proper message therefore is "no use"; on the other side is the recommendation to aim at "responsible use."

This lack of consensus is worth considering in the shaping of policies toward alcohol. Cleveland school officials, the report pointed out, are not in any disagreement with those who call alcohol use wrong and harmful. These school people who cooperated with the report pointed out that students are taught that for persons under the legal drinking age the use of alcohol is illegal. But they added that for adults alcohol is legal, and society in general accepts responsible alcohol use. Because of the relative ease with which adolescents experiment with the use of alcohol, the sensible, or at least pragmatic, course, then, is to teach them to use alcohol responsibly.

Other school officials who opposed the Cleveland testimony expressed the strong belief that the "responsible use" message clashes with the goal of drug-free schools. They maintained that schools should not convey such a message about a substance that, for students, is illegal.

The GAO's comment on this disagreement is that "the potential effectiveness of alcohol education appears to be influenced by the social acceptability of alcohol use among adults. Although most students to whom we spoke were in programs with a 'no use' message, they, too, had mixed views about the use of alcohol. Most generally agreed with school officials that alcohol is a big problem among students and adults, but most also said that alcohol was socially acceptable. Many students had the misconception that alcohol is less harmful than illicit drugs, such as cocaine or marijuana."

The students were, of course, justified in pointing to alcohol's social acceptability. Moreover, as long as alcohol is socially acceptable, it will be used and served regularly by teenagers' parents in their homes, in some cases on a daily basis, in others at social occasions.

Apart from the moral right or wrong in this matter (the history of Prohibition throws an unmistakable light on the national point of view), it is difficult for adults to make as strong an argument about alcohol as about illegal drugs. Schools do, of course, have the responsibility to prohibit alcohol use on their premises (or at least during school hours) and to penalize any infraction of the rule. Schools also would do well to teach their students about the dangers of alcohol.

In some modified ways, these distinctions between the use of alcohol and illegal drugs also apply to cigarette smoking. As already noted, human damage caused by the habit and its inevitable addiction has been proven beyond the shadow of a doubt, and such damage is compounded when smoking is begun at an early age. Every effort must be made to dissuade young people from exposing themselves to this risk. Teachers, parents, peers, community leaders—all have a responsibility to prevent smoking among children and adolescents; but as long as cigarettes are legal, widely advertised, and easily available, an outright prohibition is simply not practicable. However, schools should be made smoke free for teachers as well as for students. It is up to parents to make homes smoke free as well; but it is foolish to try to do so effectively unless the adults include themselves in the ban.

None of these distinctions in any way argues against a firm and urgent response to the ravages of every form of substance abuse. Some of the more objectionable political rhetoric—the "War on Drugs," for example, or the simplistic exhortation "Just Say No"—invites simplistic answers. The reality is complex. There is no magic bullet. Neither permissiveness nor getting tough can solve problems that, in some form, are as old as civilization. Today, illegal drugs are pushed by multibillion-dollar cartels, and alcohol and cigarettes are promoted by well-financed advertising experts with consummate skill at creating and sustaining the dangerous attraction among their young adolescent customers.

How, then, *shall* a move away from substance abuse among young adolescents be effectively promoted? For those young people who have dropped out of school, for whom the hope for gainful employment is particularly dim, the lure of the street and the escape into alcohol and drugs become stronger with every wasted day. Home often reinforces the negative—a family under stress whose adult members may be too exhausted or emotionally drained to offer guidance or nurturing, or who are already victims of drugs or alcoholism. Once adolescents have not only dropped out of school but have removed themselves from the company of those who still strive for success within the rules and laws of society, they drift toward peers who share their depression and alienation. They are easy prey for adults who stand to gain by promising them relief and happiness through drugs.

Government policy on illegal drugs over the past decade has concentrated on international interdiction and domestic policing as the major means of cutting off supply. Such a superficially militant strategy thrives on publicity. It gives the appearance of strength. But with the large amounts of money already expended and the frequent complicity by foreign military leaders and even governments themselves in feeding the supply of drugs, the emphasis on interdiction has been shown to have at best only a minor effect. The fundamental questions are still Can the demand be substantially lowered? Can society's attitudes toward addictive substances be changed?

Fortunately, there are positive signs that such changes can be achieved. Despite the propaganda efforts by the tobacco industry and the continued government support of tobacco production, for example, a marked decrease has taken place in the per-capita smoking of cigarettes.

A 1984 analysis by the Rand Corporation, which considered international and domestic policing of drugs essential, nevertheless concluded that the most serious gap in any successful drug use prevention policy is the lack of effective programs to prevent adolescents from being drawn to drugs.

How effective are existing programs? Drug abuse education courses exist in many secondary schools and in some elementary schools, but they have not been able to prevent the use of drugs by large numbers of young people. The GAO report found that little is known about the effectiveness of these various drug education programs. The 1989 amendments to the Drug-Free Schools and Communities Act called for more state and local evaluation of ongoing programs.

The act, which was passed in 1986, provides federal assistance to establish drug abuse education and prevention programs. Of the $1.3 billion Congress has since appropriated, $1.1 billion was distributed to states in the form of grants, largely to establish drug-free schools. But the GAO found that evaluations over the past five years have not demonstrated conclusively what works. As is the case with early adolescent pregnancy, it appears that simply supplying students with greater knowledge about drugs does not necessarily lead to corresponding changes in their behavior. Information alone is not enough.

On the encouraging side, the GAO found that nearly all the students surveyed, when asked about the drug education offered to them, considered it useful and believed that, without it, more students would use and sell drugs. At the same time, the students pointed to many programs' limitations. Drug education, they said, cannot change the easy availability of drugs or substantially reduce the peer pressure that makes it difficult to resist drugs and alcohol. Their leading criticism was that the education programs did not cover the subject of drug selling—a problem, they said, that was as prevalent as drug use itself. Students suggested that drug education programs should include scheduled after-school social activities as an alternative to life on the streets with its temptation of drug use. This reflects the widespread agreement among young people themselves that after-school programs in safe and congenial locations, concentrating on teenage fun, could make a real difference, especially among the poor. Such programs for young adolescents are considered crucial in many countries, especially in Scandinavia, where "discovery playgrounds" for mixed age groups and after-school "clubs" provide a wide range of activities from the arts and sports to motorcycle repair shops.

One serious obstacle to the implementation of drug education programs, the GAO study found, was the lack of trained teachers. For example, in the Detroit district in the survey, the goal was to provide a particular program for all youngsters from kindergarten through eighth grade; but because of the shortage of teachers, only half of the district's schools could actually participate. Detroit reported that only 20,254, or 11 percent, of its 176,861 students had a chance to take part in the program. In Cleveland, youngsters from kindergarten through fifth grade were targeted, but fewer than half were reached. Implementation of the programs in other districts, including Miami's Dade County and Los Angeles, was similarly spotty.

Perhaps some of these sad deficiencies are the inevitable consequence of a late start in addressing the problem. The recent increase in public discussion of education as a means of preventing drug use is a welcome change; yet, there is still painfully little indication of a consensus about the kind of education that can be expected to make a difference.

As noted earlier, there is a great need for life skills education as a vital component in any program that strives to be successful in responding to the crisis in adolescent health. One flaw in much current research on life skills education is that it has concentrated on schools with a predominantly middle-class population. There is an urgent need now to extend research and action to schools in poor communities where the problems are most serious. Disadvantaged adolescents are in most need of the life skills that will allow them to function successfully in the mainstream of society. Such basic skills as making themselves well understood and communicating effectively with others quite literally become tools of both social and economic survival. They can transform alienation and aggressive, hostile attitudes into self-confidence and a sense of belonging—qualities that drug use tries, but fails, to create.

But for students to learn to communicate and to function in a social world that is often very different from their own calls for tact and understanding on the part of those who teach life skills. Because words and ideas often have different meanings for teachers and the taught, the first task is to create mutual understanding without impatience or embarrassment. Students must be listened to and treated with respect.

At the heart of life skills teaching, for all youngsters, disadvantaged and affluent alike, must be recognition that they stand on the threshold of greater independence and responsibility for their futures. The decisions they will soon have to make may have lifelong consequences for themselves and others; decisions about their education and goals, about smoking, drinking, and drugs; about the use of vehicles, and, tragically, even decisions about the use of weapons. Knowledge for the making of judgments can be taught. It is a great mistake to assume that young people will acquire these skills automatically.

What is to be taught is a process: stop and think; get information; assess the information, always consider the consequences; weigh old options, or seek out new ones; get feedback from persons whose judgment and integrity can be trusted. To learn to master the process is as important for young people who have been protected from responsibility by families in affluent circumstances as for those whose families, deprived of the assets of education and wealth, have been unable to guide them toward confidence, independence, and hope.

One in-school experiment in Lowell, Massachusetts, bears this out. In a program called City Magnet, which serves children from kindergarten to eighth grade, more than half of the school's 330 pupils came from low-income families. Described by the *New York Times* (June 19, 1991) as "the nation's first micro-society school," it has its own court system, a representative government, and a market economy. Students work as lawyers, judges, reporters, editors, bankers, and business people. They pay rent on their desks and taxes on their salaries, using the school's own paper currency. While the school also teaches all the basic subjects, students work at assigned jobs in a seventy-minute activity period after the regular school day, where they take part in running businesses or serve in the elected legislature or in the courts.

Educators consider the school's ten-year history a success story. In addition to improved academic performance, the school reports a sharp decline in discipline and behavior problems. City Magnet was founded in 1981 in response to a desegregation court order. The experiment was based on the proposals contained in *The Micro-Society School: A Real World in Miniature*, a book by George Richmond, a former Brooklyn public school teacher.

"The purpose of this program has been to help all kids to succeed, and we believe the micro-society is doing that," said George Tsapatsaris, Lowell's superintendent of schools. Since success in school has been so widely found to reduce students' involvement in behavior that places their health at risk, this approach clearly offers great promise in the battle against alcohol, drugs, and nicotine. A replica of the Lowell experiment has been opened in Yonkers, New York, and other communities are considering the school as a model.

Another successful strategy in teaching adolescents how to cope effectively with unfamiliar challenges and strange new territory in their lives was borrowed from experiences by the Peace Corps. Before volunteers were dispatched to foreign countries to confront unanticipated problems, they met with their predecessors to benefit from their experience. Adapting that technique to young adolescents, somewhat older peers give an account of how they successfully negotiated the pitfalls of growing up. Such peer counseling, mentoring, or role modeling has proven to be valuable in giving youngsters confidence and perspective as they look to their future.

Successful examples are key ingredients of such teaching: the persuasive and attractive illustration by a respected person of how to cope with stress can help adolescents deal effectively with personal problems. Substituting the elation of competency for the fleeting highs of drugs or alcohol is the goal of this strategy.

In addition to the kind of life skills training that includes peer counseling or role modeling, young people must be given an early insight into the way their bodies work, how the body interacts with its environment, and how to protect it against avoidable harm. The adaptation of Stanford University's life science curriculum, which integrates human biology, including the biological effects of harmful substances, should become the core of a middle school science curriculum. (See chapter 3.)

Currently, public service messages about substance abuse, directed at the public in general but often specifically at young people, tend to rely on either exhortation or scare techniques. Such appeals may well be of some value, especially to a public conditioned by similar messages from, for example, politicians during election campaigns. But for long-term effectiveness, lasting beyond the instant emotional reaction, leadership is needed within the scientific, educational, and medical communities to help provide the public, and particularly children and youths, with factual information that contains a credible basis in scientific research.

In matters of such importance, it is essential to get the facts straight so that the public has reason to believe that the message can be trusted. This applies in special measure to young adolescents, who are by nature skeptical of adult pronouncements. Such skepticism, in any case, is an attitude to be cherished; it should be regarded by adults as a signal to deal with young people honestly. At the same time, messages to teenagers must be easy to understand and, if they are transmitted by way of television, radio, films, or books, readily applicable to the ordinary viewer, listener, or reader. One useful example of a visually entertaining effort to get teenagers to think about such problems as drugs, alcohol, risky sexual activity, and other vital concerns is the television series "DeGrassi Junior High." "De-Grassi" faces problems head-on and leaves the search for solutions to the teenage audience.

Another successful program is Theatreworks/USA. Now in its thirty-second season, this group produces plays for teenagers and their families, laying special stress on young adolescents' problems ranging from illiteracy to drug abuse. It has presented more than 27,000 performances of plays specifically written for the teenage audience and largely performed by teenagers under professional direction. The plays and musicals, aimed at sending constructive messages while being entertaining, have reached more than twenty-three million young people in forty-nine states. The program's stated aim is to "produce theater that enhances the lives of young people, gives them hope, and inspires creative problem solving."

By contrast, warns Howard Leventhal of Rutgers, the State University of New Jersey, little is to be gained from such televised antidrug messages as the ad asserting that the effects of drugs on the brain is equivalent to frying an egg. Adolescents are more likely to ridicule such banal images than to be frightened by them, he notes.

In approaching the broad matter of preventing substance abuse, research in the United States at Stanford University, as well as in a number of other countries, has concentrated on smoking. The reason for this is twofold: early smoking is often a gateway to other substance abuse, and persuasive, easy-to-understand scientific proof of the extremely damaging consequences of long-term smoking is available. In addition, smoking can readily be shown to have immediate consequences in areas of particular interest to teenagers, such as bad breath and interference with good performance in sports. Young adolescents who find it understandably difficult to be engaged by facts about the long-term consequences of smoking, including potential illness and death, are far more readily impressed with immediate tangible damage. It is helpful to build on this kind of recognition.

Capitalizing on the natural rebelliousness of most adolescents, programs can encourage them to express their different views and to declare their independence by critically analyzing advertising messages aimed at them. Teachers, parents, and other adults can encourage adolescents to use their energy creatively by identifying and resisting the attempts by advertisers to exploit them. Discussions of this nature also offer opportunities to point out that misleading appeals by business interests, which sell harmful substances for profit, differ little from the appeals by misguided peers who also peddle them either for profit or for prestige. One effective way for schools to combine the teaching of good writing, critical thinking skills, and health-supporting habits is the analysis of advertising as part of the regular English, social studies, or science curriculum.

The school-based approach to the dangers of smoking as an opening in the battle against other substance abuse is not new. During the 1970s, important research was launched at Cornell Medical College under the leadership of Gilbert Botvin to persuade middle school youngsters not to begin to smoke. Botvin found that the traditional antismoking education did not work because it failed to give young people the knowledge and the incentives to avoid smoking. He set out to give junior high school students the facts and to encourage reason-based attitudes along with specific skills to enable them to resist the influences that would make smokers of them.

The curriculum developed for the program stresses the kind of learning that helps young people respond to problems they confront, particularly how to resist the temptations of tobacco, alcohol, and marijuana. These are the main objectives:

▲ Reduce students' susceptibility to social pressures to use these substances by helping them develop greater autonomy, self-esteem, and self-reliance

▲ Enable students to cope with anxiety, particularly when caused by lack of feelings of security in social situations

▲ Increase the awareness of the harmful consequences of substance use, with stress on the kind of immediate effects of special concern to teenagers

▲ Provide youngsters with accurate statistics about the actual rates of tobacco, alcohol, and marijuana use to prevent them from falling into the "everybody does it" trap

▲ Help youngsters develop healthy attitudes, persuading them that they can function well without cigarettes, drugs, and alcohol

The program calls for fifteen sessions in seventh grade, a ten-session booster in eighth grade, and another ten sessions in ninth grade. It has grown from a small pilot test to a large-scale prevention course offered to several thousand students.

Such comprehensive approaches were the key to a variety of other efforts to stop the drift into substance use before it became a major factor in young people's lives. Results from an ongoing longitudinal study published in 1990 indicate that comprehensive education programs of this nature can prevent, or substantially reduce, the use of cigarettes and marijuana in early adolescence and that they are equally successful in schools with low- and high-minority enrollment. The programs do not, however, help any youngster who is already a habitual smoker, a finding that underscores the importance of reaching children and adolescents at a very early age before harmful habits are formed.

Project ALERT by the Rand Corporation, an intervention begun in 1984 in thirty schools in California and Oregon, starts in seventh grade. Two-thirds of the schools follow a smoking-, alcohol-, and drug-prevention curriculum. One-third of the schools get no special instruction and are used for comparison. In half of the schools that use the intervention, the instruction is given by an adult alone; in the other half, the adult is assisted by teenage leaders. The seventh-grade instruction consists of eight lessons, dealing with motivation to resist drug and alcohol use, the serious consequences of such use, skills to resist pressures, and the benefits of resisting them.

In the eighth grade, three booster sessions try to reinforce what has already been taught. Throughout the programs, there are opportunities for role playing, small-group discussions, and practice in how best to resist the lures of alcohol, drugs, and cigarettes. The overwhelming majority of the students who took part in the program called it credible, considered themselves actively involved, and found it helpful in their own efforts to resist pressures to use drugs. A discouraging result, however, was that the project's initial success in preventing adolescent drinking did not survive for any length of time. Despite such limitations, Project ALERT deserves attention in the battle against high-risk behavior by young adolescents.

From the results of these and other such studies, it quickly becomes evident that the battle against high-risk adolescent behavior cannot be fought by the schools alone, without parallel help and reinforcement by the community and society at large. The relative success in reducing adolescent smoking is in large part attributable to the fact that American society as a whole has turned its back on cigarettes and has been quite vocal about it. This has put smokers on the defensive. Indeed, it has led many children to chide their cigarette-addicted parents, giving youngsters a feeling of pride as defenders of healthy habits.

Another opportunity that could be seized to persuade adolescents to shun drugs, cigarettes, and alcohol is their serious interest in the protection of the environment. It is to this new generation's great credit that it has awakened, far more sensitively than many of its elders, to the dangers of the pollution of air and water and of the depletion of forests and parkland. Such concerns among the young virtually cry out to their elders to help them make the connection between the conservation of the environment and the conservation of their own healthy human bodies and minds. Apprehension over the dangers of carbon monoxide in the air they breathe and over the threat to their health through crops affected by toxic waste or insecticides should naturally and honestly be converted into concern about such toxic substances as alcohol, nicotine, and drugs.

Expanding on such concerns, however, will not be effective if adults hide behind an attitude of "do what I say, not what I do." The child who angrily objects to a parent's smoking deserves praise, not recrimination or punishment. Teenagers' objections to their parents' smoking recently have been given even greater justification by new findings providing strong evidence that smoking by parents is harmful to their children's health. The new information was made public by the National Center for Health Statistics. Louis W. Sullivan, secretary of Health and Human Services, said: "I can't think of a more compelling reason for parents to quit smoking than insuring their children's chance for a healthy life."

Nothing is to be achieved either from celebrating minor gains in the battle against health-damaging adolescent behavior or bemoaning the dimensions of the crisis as a no-win situation. The fact is that the battle on behalf of adolescent health is not easy to win, but, at the same time, it is immensely worth fighting. The success of some of the skirmishes noted throughout this book is limited indeed, but it nevertheless should be viewed as promising. It should reinforce the belief that victory is not impossible.

As in the findings to date about early pregnancies, the lesson learned from past initiatives is that little is to be gained from a narrowly confined approach. The most promising strategy is not to concentrate exclusively on the targets—alcohol, drugs, nicotine—but rather on building teenagers' confidence in themselves, their intellectual and social competence, and consequently their hope for the future.

This also means that adults, including political leaders, have the responsibility to make young people's lives tolerable. At present, life is intolerable for many youngsters who live in poverty with families that are incapable of nurturing them and who are surrounded by adult addictions and addiction-supporting illicit commerce. And many young people who live in affluence are nevertheless lacking parental nurturing and are often exposed to a show of parental excesses.

In their report for the forthcoming volume *Adolescent Health Promotion,* Howard Leventhal and Patricia Keeshan stress the crucial importance of promoting attractive, healthy alternatives to substance abuse. They call current efforts focused on individuals largely ineffective—at the very least, short lived. They urge instead programs that take into consideration the environment in which adolescents live. Leventhal and Keeshan offer a variety of lessons. Poor minority youngsters, they say, must be shown how individuals from comparable backgrounds have "made it" in legitimate, socially acceptable ways. They must become aware that retail and professional establishments run by legitimate managers, doctors, lawyers, and educators from minority communities exist as a realistic alternative to the dominant image of the "successful" drug dealer.

"Given that money and material incentives serve as primary indicators of status and success in our society, it should come as no surprise that youngsters may prefer the entrepreneurial tasks of selling heroin and crack to the tasks of studying mathematics and English as steps toward careers as engineers, physicians, or teachers," the authors say. "The media do not focus on these alternative careers, government does not support the educational systems that prepare young people to enter them, and the representatives of these careers are largely absent from the adolescents' life space."

To offer genuine alternatives to drug use and the drug trade, greater efforts are needed to give adolescents a clearer understanding of the skills and efforts required to take advantage of these alternatives. But they must also be persuaded, by example rather than exhortation, that the rewards these alternative routes promise are not arbitrary and not dependent on "whom you know" or on corruption. Unless young people can be shown that there are legitimate ways to success, high-risk behavior will continue to look attractive. Underwriting effective education and assigning value and high status to performance can pave the road for alternatives to drugs but only if the offer is genuine and the resources are sufficient to support it.

Unless adolescents from poor neighborhoods can be attracted to the alternative road to success, they will increasingly create their own substitute society of gangs, drugs, and violence, their own music, sexual ethics, and even their own language. "If a community cannot rid its parks and streets of drug peddlers and their clients, and rid itself of random violence and shootings . . . the possibility for creating alternatives to drug use will remain little more than a hoped-for fiction," Leventhal and Keeshan observe. Even youngsters who are growing up in a high-risk environment must be able to see nearby—not just in romanticized television segments—some blocks where families have fathers and mothers, where streets are not strewn with garbage, and where playgrounds are safe.

The community involvement required in such a campaign includes public and private organizations, the media, policy makers, public health authorities, private business, religious bodies, and family groups. Public health and medical institutions could dramatically show adolescents the ravages of drugs by encouraging them to visit patients who are suffering the consequences of drug abuse.

Equally important is the creation of strong links between adolescents and adults, particularly through membership in youth-serving organizations. (See chapter 7.)

For youngsters from middle- and upper-income families, substance abuse often results from the alienation engendered by parents who are cold, angry, confused, or permissive and from a teenager's lack of opportunities to use their time and energies constructively. Though we prefer to believe that affluence insulates young people from substance abuse, the evidence to the contrary is everywhere around us.

So is the evidence that nurturing makes the difference. Asked on the "MacNeil/Lehrer NewsHour" (April 9, 1991) about ways of reducing crime, and particularly drug-related crimes, committed by young people, Angel Rodriguez, a community youth worker, said: "I've done this since 1978, and my record is pretty clear. . . . If you can show some love, concern, and affection to youngsters who are not used to that, you can make a difference in their lives. . . . When a kid sees me before the bench discussing his future with a judge; with a prosecutor and his lawyer, and then sees me on his street, I think that there is an element of some empowerment in that somebody is looking out for them."

Beyond the funding of realistic school programs and organized after-school activities, business, industry, and local government can help by opening up part-time internships, apprenticeships, and community service to help make the connection between the time of transition and the world of work. We need no further evidence to show that the task for school and society is to find ways for young people to build confidence in themselves, to earn the respect of their peers and adults, and to create a circle of friends and supporters who can endorse their efforts to face the future undamaged by destructive habits and health-threatening behavior. It is in large measure the responsibility of adults, especially those with power over the reform and management of society, to give adolescents a vision of a future worth preparing for and a justified faith in a nation that delivers what it promises.

CHAPTER FIVE

DEATH AND VIOLENCE

K evin's mother, according to *U.S. News & World Report* (April 8, 1991), "was a drug addict, his father a dope dealer. After being taken from them by social workers in his native Massachusetts, Kevin went to live with his grandparents in Texas. His grandfather, a security guard, let him shoot a .22, and 'firing made me feel like I was on top.' By his early teens, he was firing a gun out windows at a nearby day-care center to show off and he had joined a gang. He began carrying a .38-caliber revolver at fourteen and obtained guns by burglarizing nearby homes. 'I wanted to carry a weapon because I wasn't going to tolerate anything.' At fifteen, Kevin began working for a Jamaican drug trafficking posse and eventually became an enforcer who did his work by shooting people in the arm."

In 1987, according to the National Center for Health Statistics, homicide was the third leading cause of death for persons ten to nineteen years of age. In that same year, one of sixteen adolescents was a victim of violent crimes — a total of 1,728,120, or 6.2 percent of the age group, according to the Federal Bureau of Investigation.

In the rate of homicides, American adolescents are at much higher risk for being victims of gun-inflicted injury or death than are adolescents in four other industrial countries (Japan, Germany, Australia, and Canada). In the majority of instances in which guns were reported to be owned by adolescents, they

were gifts from relatives, usually a father, grandfather, uncle, or older brother. The median age of first gun ownership was twelve and a half. As will be noted later, U.S. weapons laws tend to be both confused and permissive. For instance, in North Carolina, gifts of guns are illegal only if the recipient child is under twelve years of age.

Such general observations, however, still do not effectively convey the true dimension of the violence that now haunts the lives of so many young adolescents.

▲ The principal of an inner-city junior high school in New York apologized for not having returned a call for three days. "These have been rough days," she explained. Three of her pupils had been shot, one of them shot to death across the street from the school.

▲ A thirteen-year-old boy was shot and killed in a Bronx apartment when a gun that was being handed around among friends fired by accident. The incident happened only hours after a girl, aged thirteen, was shot and wounded when a semiautomatic gun, also being handled by friends, accidentally fired.

▲ In August 1990, a fifteen-year-old boy in Brooklyn who worked as a gunman for a ring of crack dealers shot and critically wounded a three-year-old girl who was playing on the sidewalk. She was the tenth child under the age of thirteen to be shot within a two-month period. Five of the children died.

▲ In the same month, a three-week-old baby boy in New York was shot to death in his crib when a gun his father was cleaning accidentally went off.

▲ On May 10, 1991, in Queens, two fourteen-year-olds, a boy and a girl, were arrested after they threatened another fourteen-year-old with a gun.

▲ Three Brooklyn teenagers, two aged fifteen and the third sixteen, were charged with killing a grocery store owner in an attempted holdup.

▲ During one month in 1991, twenty-four youngsters sixteen or younger were shot in New York, five of them fatally. The last of

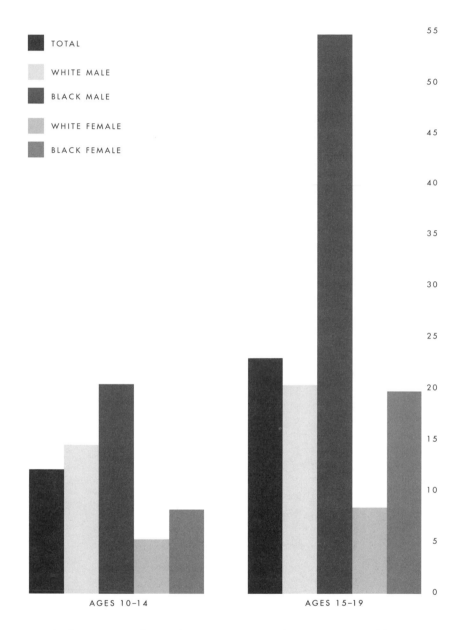

Deaths from Firearms for Adolescents 10 to 14 and 15 to 19 Years Old, 1989

PERCENTAGE OF ALL DEATHS

Source: National Center for Health Statistics. Data computed by L. A. Fingerhut, Division of Analysis. Data compiled by the Division of Vital Statistics.

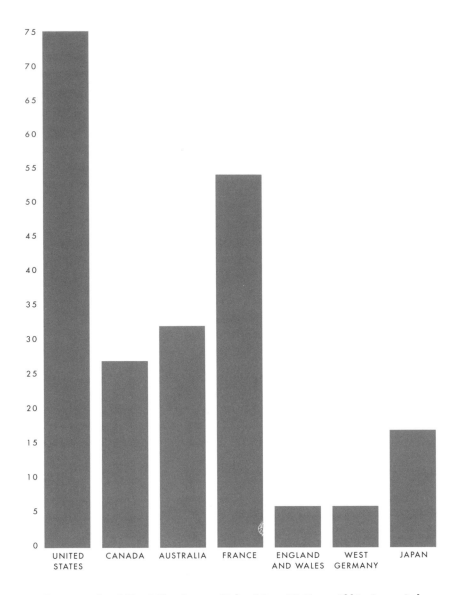

Firearm-related Homicides Among Males 15 to 24 Years Old in Seven Industrialized Nations, 1986 and 1987

FIREARM-RELATED HOMICIDES AS A PERCENTAGE OF ALL HOMICIDES

Source: L. A. Fingerhut and J. C. Kleinman (1990). "International and Interstate Comparisons of Homicide Among Young Males," *Journal of the American Medical Association* 263 (24): 3292–95.

the victims, fifteen, was struck by gunfire as he tried to avoid a fight at a high school in Queens.

▲ In Oakland, California, a twelve-year-old boy was charged with homicide for killing a drug dealer. Jane Gross, reporting in the *New York Times* (May 26, 1991), wrote: "While the crime he is charged with is extraordinary, the twelve-year-old is in many ways typical of the children of America's inner cities: reared by a single mother, searching for male role models and living in neighborhoods where drugs and guns are everywhere and economic and educational opportunities are rare."

Don Sutton, coordinator for the Oakland Crack Task Force, commented: "We are definitely in a war for these kids. For some of them, people who sell drugs are the only male images they see." He added: "The system is set up to create youngsters like this.... The school system is cut back. The recreation programs? They're mostly gone. The extended family doesn't hardly exist anymore.... If we know they're hanging out in the street, what do we think they're getting involved with?"

Without the shadow of a doubt, teenage violence has become a major public health and safety issue. The *Wall Street Journal* on March 25, 1991, quite accurately called it an epidemic in a front-page article that started with a report of the killing by a fifteen-year-old of his best friend, aged fourteen, in an argument over a girl.

For many young people, violence has become a terrifying and constant presence. Researchers at the University of Maryland's School of Medicine asked 168 teenagers who were visiting an inner-city clinic about their experience with violence. Twenty-four percent said they had witnessed a murder; 72 percent knew somebody who had been shot. Two out of five black children on Chicago's South Side reported having witnessed a shooting, and one-fourth had actually seen a murder. Such early traumatic experiences deeply affect youngsters' view of life.

Lawrence Gary, director of the Institute for Urban Affairs and Research at Howard University, refers to adolescent violence as a new phenomenon in America, even within the context of this country's history of violence. In many inner cities, homicide has become the leading cause of death among children. Blacks suffer the most serious impact of the epidemic. In 1988, more than 1,000 black children and adolescents were victims of homicide, an increase of 50 percent since 1985.

The Forum on Youth Violence in Minority Communities provides this overview of the crisis: in New York City, acquiring a gun has become a "rite of passage" among adolescents at high risk of committing or suffering violence. In Washington, D.C., serious injuries, especially from handguns, among youngsters seen at Children's Hospital have increased 1,500 percent since 1986. Trauma centers show a 300 percent increase in admissions for gunshot wounds among people under the age of eighteen, most of whom were shot by youngsters of sixteen or less.

Forty-one percent of the juveniles held for violent crimes had used a weapon, most frequently a gun. Each gun injury is five times more likely to result in death than an injury from the next most deadly weapon, a knife. In California, from July 1988 to June 1989, schools confiscated 10,569 weapons, an increase of 21 percent over the past year. In Baltimore, a court study found that of 390 high school students polled, 64 percent knew someone who had been shot, threatened, or robbed at gunpoint in school, and almost all the boys said they had carried a handgun to school at least once.

In inner-city Boston, a middle-class mother not only restricts her child's play outside but forbids him to stand near windows while indoors. Another parent comments that he's glad to live on a dead-end street because children can play there without fear of drive-by shootings.

In Los Angeles, Melba Coleman, principal of an inner-city elementary school, holds a daily safety drill in the school yard. The exercises are an adaptation of the 1950s "duck and cover" nuclear attack drill, but this time they are held to help protect the youngsters from the actual and continuing reality of neighborhood violence. Ronald Stephens, executive director of the federally financed National School Safety Center, says such drills are becoming prevalent around the country.

Young black males face the most serious threat of harm to life and limb. They are seven times more likely than white youths to die as a result of homicide, according to 1988 data compiled by the National Center for Health Statistics. The rates for American Indian and Hispanic youths were about three to four times that of whites; that for Asians was virtually the same as for whites.

Yet, according to a report by the Contra Costa Health Services Department in California, the statistics about homicide tell only part of the story: according to conservative estimates, for every homicide there are 100 largely unreported assaults. Sexual assaults are even more regularly hidden from public view. The rate of reported rapes increased by 21 percent between the years of 1977 and 1984.

The Police Foundation comments: "Inner-city residents disproportionately share in the misery resulting from crime and fear of crime. The entrepreneurial talents and skills of some of the brightest youngsters residing in the inner cities are employed in the lucrative trade of manufacturing and distributing intoxicating substances. Boys and girls join associations that traffic illegal narcotics through sophisticated networks of beeper-carrying couriers. They war with each other, deface buildings, terrorize neighborhoods, and engage in other malicious acts. . . . And too frequently, bloody, bruised, and battered bodies are placed on cold slabs in city-run morgues."

The institutionalization of violence among our young people is producing a new economy. There is a jacket for children on the market, and it costs $500. What makes the jacket so expensive is its lining: a flexible sheet of Kevlar capable of stopping a 9-mm slug from a semiautomatic gun. Designed by a former police officer turned security consultant, it is advertised as "the latest for the urban kid in this era of drive-by shootings." Perhaps the cynical creation of a smart entrepreneur, the jacket is nevertheless a reflection of a legitimate fear: children are being hurt and murdered by drive-by killers. The fact: every thirty-six minutes a child is killed or injured by a gun, adding up to more than 14,000 children a year.

In 1989, the *Boston Globe* reported that "when you go into a Boston high school and ask how many kids know of someone who has died of homicide, nearly all the hands go up." The question would elicit the same response in the classrooms of many American cities. The Education Development Center in Massachusetts comments: "Increasingly, the analogy is being drawn between life in America's poor urban neighborhoods and the battle zones of such countries as Lebanon, Northern Ireland, Afghanistan and Burma."

At Thomas Jefferson High School in Brooklyn, there is a "grieving room." It was set up when a ninth-grade boy was killed and the children needed a place where students could cry together and comfort each other.

In Chicago, Diana F. Barone, a popular fourth-grade teacher whose experience is described briefly in Alex Kotlowitz's book, *There Are No Children Here,* had been worn down by the relentless violence: "The parking lot behind the school had been the site of numerous gang battles. When the powerful sounds of .357 magnums and sawed-off shotguns echoed off the school walls, the streetwise students slid off their chairs and huddled under their desks. This was merely their sensible reaction to the possibility of bullets flying through the window. Barone, along with other teachers, placed the back of her chair against a pillar so that there would be a solid object between herself and the window.

"She dreaded the walk each morning and afternoon from and to her car. . . . She regularly slipped her paycheck into her bra before making the short trek to her car."

Violence is not confined to inner cities. It occurs increasingly in suburbs, small towns, and rural settings. Wherever it happens, however, the segment of the population most likely to be victimized, most likely to commit violent crimes, and most likely to be arrested are youths. On any given day, approximately 100,000 adolescents are confined in correctional institutions.

All of this should not obscure the fact that the majority of children, adolescents, and adults living in inner-city neighborhoods are law abiding and nonviolent. They want to go about their business—attending school in the case of most of the youngsters—in peace. They try as hard as they can to stay away from threatening situations. Unless they are defeated early by hopelessness, the majority of disadvantaged young people have the same aspirations as their more affluent contemporaries.

It is abhorrent that adolescents are continually exposed to the violence and the gunfire that threaten their peace of mind and their very lives. It is intolerable that in a democratic society some of its members should be at such serious risk; that young people, instead of looking forward to growing up, must concentrate those precious years on trying to survive a lethal environment. Because these violent realities are so painful, there is a tendency to turn away from them or to accept them as the normal consequences of modern urban America. In fact, there is nothing normal about such violence; it calls for drastic efforts to put an end to the mayhem, to negotiate and enforce domestic arms control, and to actively protect the right of children and youths to grow up unharmed.

THE SOURCES OF ADOLESCENT VIOLENCE

Drugs and gangs are surely major factors in spreading the epidemic of violence among young people, but the disintegration of the family, particularly but not exclusively in areas of urban poverty, is a major root of the crisis. The absence of fathers from so many homes places an intolerable burden on women, particularly poor women, as heads of households. Under these stressful circumstances, in inner-city neighborhoods, the male role models for young people often are the lawless, unemployed young men on the street, the high-income drug dealer, the juvenile leader of a gang, or a mother's irresponsible, and often violent, sex partner.

Gang membership often makes daily life more tolerable for vulnerable young people. Tony Ostos, of the local Department of Human Services of Paramount, California, challenges the general public's view of gangs when he notes that most people think of gang members as tall, threatening guys riding motorcycles or peering out menacingly from street corners. In reality, he explains, "we found that young people become interested in gang membership around the age of eleven. These are kids!" Their dismal surroundings and their sense of isolation pull them into gangs in their search for a place where they feel wanted, protected, and respected.

As a result, gangs have been growing at an alarming rate, alarming because gang members often engage in violence and gunfire in order to "prove" themselves. Conflicts that used to end in fistfights are now increasingly resolved with the use of deadly knives and guns. Often shots are fired over the acquisition of material goods—leather jackets, running shoes, stereos—or as a tragic, ritualized response to a verbal slight or "show" of disrespect. "Dissing," the slang expression for any affront to a youngster's "reputation," can be the cause for a teenage death sentence. And such death sentences are carried out with terrifying frequency as disadvantaged young people, cut off from the possibilities of mainstream success, create their own brutal societies.

As youngsters prove themselves in the handling of firearms, they are hired by adults as runners in the drug trade. The adult criminal knows that minors are treated more leniently by the courts and thus make desirable, often deadly, assistants to merchants and enforcers. For the youngsters, the lure is a combination of easy money, a sense of usefulness, and hero worship of the successful dealer. It is not without significance that in street language "bad" is a term of admiration.

The number of minors arrested for murder increased by 31 percent between 1983 and 1988, for a total of 1,765. Of that total, 201 were young adolescents of fourteen or younger. Victor Herbert, formerly one of New York City's most successful high school principals, commented about the trend: "There's real fear among young people about each other."

Many public housing projects are particularly vulnerable to violence. Because the projects contain large numbers of disadvantaged people with a variety of problems, they often become havens for drug use and sale. This situation poses a severe threat to the majority of project residents who want only to lead safer, peaceful lives but live in constant fear that they and their children will become victims of the violence that accompanies drug dealing.

Like many public schools, the projects suffer from the damaging consequences of great size. The ensuing sense of anonymity that destroys a feeling of community makes it difficult to form neighborly ties. For teenagers this is a special threat. *Turning Points* emphasized the crucial importance of close personal links between every adolescent and at least one caring, reliable adult. The lack of such contacts in the impersonal and often threatening atmosphere of the housing projects creates serious risks for youngsters growing up in them.

The combination of such danger-prone conditions and one-parent homes under stress escalates child abuse of every kind—physical, psychological, and sexual. Violence against children and adolescents at the hands of mothers' sex partners, and even by drug- and alcohol-addicted mothers themselves, is identified by many researchers as evoking, in turn, violence by the teenagers raised in such an environment. Again, violent behavior is hardly confined to inner cities; affluent families are simply better able to conceal its ravages, unless they occasionally break out in headlines.

When children grow up as witnesses to aggression between family members, they may conclude that to resort to brute force is an acceptable part of family and social life. In extreme cases, such as severe injuries inflicted on—or even a murder of—a parent, the trauma and the distortion of personal values turn the children into victims, rather than mere observers.

A predominantly black elementary school in the Watts section of Los Angeles tried to counteract the damage done among children who have witnessed such violence by developing a "grief-and-loss" class taught by a psychiatric social worker. The class utilizes field trips, gardening, and games to encourage children to talk about their feelings. It features reading books aloud about death and engages the children in creative arts projects. The aim is twofold: to help the children overcome the grief and the shock of their experience and to prevent them from adopting similarly violent, antisocial behavior later.

While youngsters who have grown up in a violent environment are obviously at greater risk of accepting violence as a normal pattern of life inside and outside the family, children are also extremely resilient. Given proper guidance and understanding, they can be led out of the morass of physical and psychological aggression. They must be taught that all people have feelings and that their own attitudes and actions not only affect others but can powerfully influence the way other people treat them. Once learned, these dynamics of everyday communication offer gratifying alternatives to violent, aggressive behavior. But these teachings must be grounded in genuine and credible support that offers hope for the future.

Current research shows that physical punishment in dealing with young children is approved and applied four times more often in poor families than in more affluent ones. Corporal punishment often is akin to, and may be indistinguishable from, abuse. National surveys of more than 3,000 parents show that children are spanked most often at the early ages of three or four. Children who are being punished in this way, or who are the victims of violence by older siblings, are given a memorable demonstration of aggression that teaches them that the use of force is accepted social behavior. These children usually are smart enough not to lash out against their parents, but they may act aggressively against other, usually smaller, children. Since they were first victimized by family members to whom they are attached in terms of dependency and love, such punishment may suggest that love and violence are compatible.

Beleaguered social service agencies and schools often lack the personnel and resources to detect or prevent child abuse. It is only when violent, usually drug-induced, abuse by middle-class parents causes the death of a child that public attention is focused on the awful truth and sustained for any period of time. Many similar crimes, committed daily against unprotected youngsters in their own homes, go largely unreported and ignored.

Can the schools emerge as safe havens for children trying to escape violence? Tragically, the schoolhouse is no longer a sanctuary. Each month, nearly 300,000 high school students are physically attacked, many in, or on the way to, school. Sandra Feldman, president of New York City's United Federation of Teachers, observes: "If we can't ensure at least inside a school building or school yard that there is still safety from the chaos of the streets, then I fear for the future of our whole society."

For the moment, such safety appears to be a vain hope for students in too many schools. The National Adolescent Student Health Survey estimates, based on a 1987 study, that 338,000 students nationwide carried a handgun to school at least once during that year and that a third of them did so every day. About eight times as many are thought to carry knives. Many of them, when asked, would say that they are arming themselves only for their own protection; nevertheless, their resort to weaponry is as dangerous as when the same rationale is offered by law-abiding adults. Contrary to the National Rifle Association's often-repeated statement that people, not guns, kill people, the fact, proven again and again, is that guns, merely by being available, kill people. Many of those people are children and adolescents. When firearms are readily available to adults for self-protection, they are also readily available to children.

Domestic gun use has a brief and violent history in the United States. The introduction of the handgun by Samuel Colt in 1840 made domestic violence more lethal. This easily concealed weapon combined the elements of speed, surprise, and finality as an ultimate arbiter in the settlement of disputes. A century and a half later, matters have been made infinitely worse with the addition of automatic assault weapons.

The National Adolescent Health Survey found that 41 percent of boys and 24 percent of girls report that they could obtain a handgun if they wanted one. Present gun control laws, which are not backed by any nationwide, federal regulations, are woefully ineffective. In cities with strong local laws, such as Boston, New York, and Washington, weapons are routinely imported from outside and sold at a profit in street trading. *U.S. News & World Report* (April 8, 1991) told of two men in Los Angeles who, operating out of a van, were estimated to have sold more than 1,000 handguns in an eight-month period in 1990. Police reported that in suburban Chicago a sixteen-year-old boy rented a gun from a fellow student for $100 and used it to kill his parents.

Children and adolescents often obtain guns that are carelessly left in accessible places in their homes. A Florida school study showed that 86 percent of the guns confiscated by school authorities had actually come from the students' homes.

Researchers studying the case histories of eighty-eight California children up to age fourteen who were fatally shot by other children or by themselves between 1977 and 1983 found that most of these incidents occurred while the youngsters were playing with loaded guns they had found. Handguns were involved in 58 percent of these cases. Under the age of eight, many children cannot distinguish a real gun from a toy.

A 1989 poll reported that nearly three out of five Americans own guns. Domestic firearm production, after briefly declining in the 1980s, again rose steadily from 3.1 million in 1986 to 4.4 million in 1989. Efforts to stop the slaughter and the fear of violence by controlling the sale and possession of guns continue to be blocked by the gun lobby's claim that the constitution guarantees all citizens the right to bear arms. The fact that the Constitutional guarantee was intended to uphold only the right of the states to maintain an armed citizen militia is generally ignored by gun rights advocates.

In desperation, after much violent gun play in his jurisdiction, Vince Lane, chairman of Chicago's Housing Authority, decided to enforce a twenty-year-old provision to bar all guns from the Rockwell Gardens Development, a housing project. He reported on the "MacNeil/Lehrer NewsHour" (June 13, 1991) that he authorized the confiscation of all guns within the project "so that we can make it a normal community environment where these kids can go to school without being harassed." Despite a great deal of community support, however, Lane ran into instant opposition, as well as a lawsuit, mounted by the National Rifle Association (NRA). Richard Gardiner, a spokesman for the NRA, said that, even though the housing project had reported seventy-one murders in 1990, people should not be deprived of their guns because "firearms are a very useful tool for self-defense" and that the "fundamental right" to own guns must be upheld.

Chief Leroy Martin of the Chicago Police Department replied in anger: "I wish the NRA would come and purchase this building and then we can let all the gun-toters and pistoleers move in here. Tell 'em to buy it. . . . They're the lobby for the manufacturers of guns, and they want to sell guns because they make money. The NRA couldn't give a damn about these people living in these housing projects. . . . "

The Chicago conflict and the frustration over the roadblock in the way of disarming a troubled and violent housing project represents, in microcosm, the national dilemma. The elimination of unlicensed guns is essential to the protection of American adolescents as the first step toward a safe, nonviolent future.

Without urgent, drastic action toward truly effective gun control, violence will escalate. James O'Kane, a criminologist and professor of sociology at Drew University in New Jersey, points out that, in response to growing danger in the streets, more people are arming themselves. As a result, he says, "teenagers are armed for defensive purposes. They're afraid that somebody is going to attack them. They carry a weapon, are packing a gun. . . . Someone gets into an argument—could be someone's a Mets fan and someone's a Yankee fan. An argument breaks out. The next thing you know, you have a dead body."

PREVENTING VIOLENCE

I n 1990, Carnegie Corporation of New York funded the Education Development Center, Inc., to hold a conference that would try to identify violence prevention programs for adolescents between the ages of ten and fifteen. At the meeting's conclusion, the participants admitted that "violence prevention as a field and in its specific activities remains poorly understood." They urged greater efforts to "sell" the need for action by focusing on violence "as one of the most serious, life-threatening, injury-producing dysfunctional forms of problem behavior."

David A. Hamburg, the Corporation's president, summarized the urgency: "My belief is that we surely do have enough knowledge, evidence, and experience now to do things better than we are at the present time."

When fear stalks the halls of a school or the streets to and from school, education is also a victim. Fortunately, some educators refuse to surrender. Deborah Meier, director of Central Park East Secondary School in East Harlem, has made a commitment to achieving a school that is violence free. The rules are strict, and everybody understands that they must be obeyed. Paul Schwarz, the school's codirector, comments on the success of the antiviolence program: "People do not expect violence. Students feel safe." The rules simply state that there is to be no fighting, not even as a game. There is to be no threat of fighting, and in the event that somebody breaks a rule, no "fighting back," either on or off school grounds. The only exception that allows a student to fight back is if his or her life is in jeopardy.

While the rules matter, even more important is the fact of

their acceptance by the entire school community and the insistence by the adults that the rules will be obeyed. But a safe and effective school must first be a community.

The school's adults realize that the policy of nonviolence and nonaggression is not without risks. It hits a raw nerve in people who believe that fighting, and "fighting back," is part of growing up.

Schwarz is not impressed by this point of view. He recalls the bumper sticker "What if they gave a war and no one came?" Deborah Meier explains the basis of the school's policy: "Maybe mutual respect is what we're all looking for."

What if students are attacked outside the school? Not even the most effective community inside can eliminate that threat. The only acceptable answer can be the creation of violence- and drug-free zones in a wide radius around schools and on the routes that youngsters must take to get to and from school. In the present climate, it is clear that school-crossing guards cannot begin to exert such influence. City authorities must provide and enforce these safety cordons, and they must strictly enforce the laws against weapons and drugs. Old rules that prohibit the presence of bars near schools seem quaint holdovers from less dangerous days; today, danger, lurks on the streets, and it is often fatal.

Parents, of course, bear a special responsibility for protecting their children's physical and psychological safety. And yet, as children grow into adolescence, their parents' ability to protect them becomes more limited. Stephen A. Small of the Department of Child and Family Studies at the University of Wisconsin points out, for example, that while parents of young adolescents can no longer supervise their children as they walk to school, they still must monitor them and teach them how to assume greater responsibility for self-protection, including dealing with emergencies when at home alone.

In the book *How to Raise a Street-Smart Child*, Grace Hechinger makes the same point: parents must teach children specific survival precepts, such as not to be on the street at certain hours, to avoid areas of special danger, and to know places to which they can turn for help or safety.

Recapturing a sense of community is imperative for the protection of young people and society. Ivan Warner, justice of the New York State Supreme Court, noted the immense differences between America's recent past and the present. Today, he said, the people who come before him in court tell him that he does not understand the streets. And even though he himself grew up on the streets, he admits that "to a great extent they're right. It was not like this. You had something, some backdrop. We had community centers . . . we had schools, public schools open in the afternoon from three to five, open again from seven to ten, five days a week. So you had some place to throw yourself, to throw this energy, this young energy that you had, this teenage energy. . . . You didn't have an opportunity to see this pusher on the corner with the big car, with the bouncing radios . . . to adulate or to try to copy. . . . " Referring to the perspective of today's teenager on the street, Justice Warner said: "The institutions have failed. Society tells me I'm nothing, and if society continues to tell me I'm nothing and I'm nobody and I'll never be anyone, I'm going to act in that manner as a nothing."

Why should mainstream America be concerned about what happens on inner-city streets? Justice Warner answers: "Because we don't have a wall [to separate the poor from the affluent, . . . you'll] find that your children, too, are being infected. I didn't say affected. I said infected. And your family structure is being destroyed also, even with all the big bucks. . . . And the fine homes with fine lawns, they are also being destroyed. So we just cannot isolate this thing. We are one nation, whether we want to believe it or not. . . . I don't think we have any idea as to the depth of this whole problem because everyone believes that it's on the other fellow's block and not mine. That's the short-sightedness of all of us."

Recent reports confirm this. The *Wall Street Journal* (February 7, 1992) cites fatal gunplay by young teenagers in such affluent suburbs as Westport, Connecticut, and East

Hampton, New York. It quotes George Butterfield, deputy director of the National School Safety Center, on what he calls the migration of guns to suburban areas, just as drugs have come to middle-class youths. "It's just that in the suburbs you have a lot more denial," he said. In affluent communities, each violent death is called a mere accident or "an isolated incident."

There is no time to lose. A paper by Felton Earls et al., "The Control of Violence and the Promotion of Non-Violence in Adolescence," prepared for the forthcoming book on adolescent health promotion commissioned by the Carnegie Council, proposes specific intervention programs that include direct approaches to gangs and their members, the establishment of truces and safe areas, the imposition and enforcement of effective gun controls, and the promotion of alternative activities, such as national service, job training, and educational programs for youths at risk.

The paper points to "the unhappy cycle of failure that begins in childhood" and that accelerates in adolescence, noting that the cycle often begins with failure in school, thereby closing off virtually all routes to employment. The authors warn:

"In the face of these barriers [easy access to guns, widespread use of alcohol and drugs, and the decay of central-city areas], an effort at health promotion may be the equivalent of trying to control an epidemic of tuberculosis in a densely populated area without adequate sanitation. Antibiotics may be of some value in treating individual cases and a vaccine may be of even greater value in protecting some groups of individuals, but the environmental conditions that promote the disease would simply overwhelm public resources in combatting it through these means. . . . What we may need to promote nonviolence as a health objective is something analogous to what was needed to control infectious diseases toward the end of the last century: vast environmental and policy changes."

Preventing aggressive and violent behavior, the authors stress, is relatively easier than trying to deal with it once it has already been established. For example, intervention with individual adolescents to treat violence-prone behavior by way of psychotherapy, behavioral therapy, or family therapy has met with only limited success, when compared to the effectiveness of such treatment begun with preadolescent children. The rate of success with adolescents is low partly because approximately one-third of these youngsters withdraw from treatment.

At the earliest stage, violence prevention begins with good health care for mother and child, minimizing violent behavior within the family, and stimulating the development of nonconfrontational skills in language and behavior. Such an approach to preschool children has already proven useful, as in the long-term effects of the Perry Preschool Project of Ypsilanti, Michigan, sponsored by the High/Scope Educational Research Foundation. Among alumni, it has led to fewer clashes with the law in the experimental group than in a control group in the adolescent years and beyond.

What other efforts could reduce violence among adolescents? Of those described briefly in what follows, none has yet been subjected to independent long-term evaluation, yet each deserves consideration. Since interest in gangs often begins at around age eleven, prevention programs must start even earlier. A curriculum entitled Alternative to Gang Membership in Paramount, California, starts in fifth grade with special classroom presentations made to students for fifteen weeks. Its units deal with such issues as graffiti, peer pressure, tattoos, the impact of gang membership on other family members, gangs and drugs, and alternatives to dangerous, health- and life-threatening behavior. The program then follows the youngsters into middle school and reaches out to get parents involved.

At the beginning of the program, 50 percent of more than 3,000 students said that they were undecided about joining a gang; at its conclusion, 90 percent said they would not. Such findings are not conclusive. Some youngsters may simply give what they feel is the "right" answer to please the instructor. And the program's success may be largely attributable to the instructor's charisma.

In 1985, a program to teach children how to resolve conflicts without violence was introduced in New York City's Community School District 15 in Brooklyn, cosponsored by the Board of Education and Educators for Social Responsibility. The program, which has since spread to more than fourteen districts and seventy schools, aims at showing children how they can use nonviolent ways of dealing with conflicts in their own lives, how they can understand and appreciate their own and other people's cultures, and how they can play a role in creating a more peaceful world.

The program contains a twenty-hour training course for teachers as well as classroom instruction and visits by expert consultants. In 1987, a student mediation component was added in five elementary schools. Most of the teachers involved praised the program. Eighty-five percent said that they were able to extend their conflict resolution training to their other lessons, although some wanted extra help in their efforts to do so. Many teachers believed that their own attitudes about conflict resolution had improved, that they were more willing to let young people take responsibility for solving their own problems, and that they had become more understanding of the childrens' concerns.

One teacher said: "In the past I have felt frustrated and incapable of helping those with a great deal of anger. As a result of the training, I can clearly see that with the tools and insight I've gained, I can facilitate a solution." Another teacher: "I now view conflict as something positive and not something that should be avoided at all costs."

The program's success among students was also promising. Between 66 and 78 percent of the participating teachers reported that students' behavior had improved and that there was less physical violence in the classroom, less name calling, fewer verbal put-downs, an increased willingness to cooperate, and a better understanding of the other person's point of view. Where student mediation was used, 535 such initiatives proved successful in a one-year period.

Overall, the results were favorable, and most participants

urged expansion of the effort. As with so many promising experiments, its potential usefulness is limited by doubts about future funding for a sufficient number of skilled personnel needed to adapt the experience to large schools, whose impersonal settings tend to be the sites of the most serious conflicts and violence.

Another promising project was put in place as an emerging measure to respond to events in Kansas City in 1977. Nine young women had been brutally murdered, and there were charges that the police were lax in seeking to apprehend the murderers because the victims were black. Citizens formed the Ad Hoc Group Against Crime and developed a program that is still in effect. Through referrals from middle and high schools, youth-serving agencies, and courts, the project identifies high-risk youths and gives them ten hours of training and counseling. A staff of volunteers reaches both males (60 percent) and females (40 percent). The majority are between ages sixteen and twenty-one, but 30 percent are as young as ten to fifteen. The program includes training in conflict resolution, anger control, problem solving, and alternatives to violence, using role playing and simulations as well as discussion and written materials. A massive public education campaign, delivered via minority-oriented radio and television programs, and a speakers' bureau try to build a climate that rejects violence and urges citizens to seek nonviolent ways of resolving disputes.

Mark Mitchell, deputy director for the city's Department of Health, notes: "Kansas City ranked ninth in the nation in homicide rates among major American cities from 1987 to 1989. Now, the homicide rate has actually dropped, instead of rising as it has in the rest of the nation. We hope this project will contribute to further decline."

Other cities are experimenting with similar strategies. In the mid-1980s, Philadelphia was suffering from alarmingly high rates of domestic violence and one of the worst gang problems in the nation. To address the threat of gangs, the Crisis Intervention Network and the Young Great Society were formed.

Former gang members patrol the city in cars looking for potential trouble in the streets as well as for conflicts they might be able to diffuse. Police join in the efforts. In one neighborhood they distribute walkie-talkies, and trained residents use them to call for help when needed. Project workers also intervene after violence has claimed its victims. In hospitals, counselors offer support and attempt to persuade those who have suffered injuries not to plan revenge, and so perpetuate violence.

Like others who are trying to stem the tide, Rudolph Sutton, Philadelphia's acting assistant health commissioner, stresses the importance of organizing to fight violence on the local level with as much community participation as possible. "We have to collect local data," he says. "Get someone to stand in the emergency room on a Saturday night, and count! Find out how much this violence is costing the community in productive years lost, in funeral expenses. Then use the data to educate politicians."

In Los Angeles, the Community Youth Gang Services works directly with gang members to settle disputes nonviolently. The strategies include agreements on "neutral" territories that are safe for everybody. The organization also tries to keep more young people in school and to open jobs for them. As in the other such experiments, evaluation of the program has been limited, but the available statistics show that gang-related homicides in areas where the services have been deployed are sharply lower. When the programs shifted away to other areas, however, homicides in the original territory quickly shot back to their original preintervention level. This proves two points: intervention can make a substantial difference, and one-shot, limited-time treatments are doomed to fail.

In Boston, Deborah Prothrow-Stith, former Massachusetts commissioner of health and now assistant dean for government and community programs at Harvard's School of Public Health, has developed and taught a tenth-grade course on preventing homicide and suicide. On the assumption that education can change behavior, she concentrates on the prevention of violence among peers and its relationship to homicide. The Violence Prevention Project, which has become a national model, stresses positive ways to deal with anger and arguments, shows how fights start and escalate, and offers nonviolent alternatives for the resolution of conflicts.

One lesson learned from the project is that intervention limited to classrooms, while useful, is not enough. The community has to become involved. Efforts initially concentrated on predominantly black Roxbury, which has the nation's highest incidence of adolescent homicide, and on predominantly white South Boston, which, with Roxbury, constitutes the city's poorest area. In each community, a trained educator carries the violence prevention curriculum to diverse audiences outside the schools: churches, housing projects, boys' and girls' clubs, neighborhood health centers, and even juvenile detention facilities, thus reaching hundreds of people.

Because the project's managers are aware that prevention messages arrive too late for the many people who have already become victims of violence, the staff tries to reach adolescents who have been admitted to Boston City Hospital with violence-engendered injuries. Unfortunately, once released, few victims come back for follow-up services. To get around that problem, pediatric nurses follow seriously injured adolescents and work with them and their families.

To help alleviate stress on the community, an organization called the Community Coalition to Prevent Black Homicide has been founded. In addition to working with specially identified schools and hospitals, the coalition turned to the media to spread the antiviolence message. In response, WGBH, Boston's public television station, ran an award-winning documentary, "Private Violence, Public Crisis."

One of the obstacles to creating and sustaining citizen action to curb violence is the sense of frustration and powerlessness to bring about social change. Prothrow-Stith comments: "Many people don't think that violence can be avoided. They accept it as an inevitable part of life. We recognize anger as a normal and potentially constructive emotion. Students have legitimate reasons for their anger—they need to respond in healthy rather than unhealthy ways. But violence is, by and large, an unhealthy way to respond. We're working to teach them better ways."

In a crisis that demands a comprehensive and urgent response, Prothrow-Stith says bluntly: "Our children are killing each other because we teach violence. We've got to do something to stop the slaughter."

If violence prevention is to be successful, she warns, the television and film industry must be reached to change its ways. At present, she charges, the industry goes out of its way to portray violence as glamorous and painless. "We had an incident at Boston City Hospital not long ago in which a thirteen-year-old kid came in with a gunshot wound," she recalls, "and he was surprised because it hurt."

The television and movie industries do indeed bear a heavy responsibility for making violence appear an acceptable, perhaps even normal, way of life. This media conditioning begins when children are at an early age, virtually in infancy. Many cartoons to which very young children are regularly exposed, often without any adult presence, include violence that is meant to amuse. The problem often is not the violent action itself but rather the fact that it does not appear to cause pain or inflict lasting damage; the person or animal flattened by a fallen rock quickly recovers his original shape without any apparent consequences. Often, too, the violence is implicitly justified by being directed by the good guys against the villains. Whatever lessons about right and wrong these battles may teach, they fall short of any suggestion that conflicts can be resolved in nonviolent fashion.

As children grow older, the message that violence is the American way intensifies. It is estimated that, by the time youngsters graduate from high school, many of them will have watched television 22,000 hours, compared to only half that number of hours spent in school. By age eighteen, young people will have been exposed to as many as 18,000 televised murders and 800 suicides.

The National Institute of Mental Health found that an average of 80.3 percent of all television programs contain violent acts, and a typical program includes 5.21 such incidents. The message of a great number of these programs is that violence is the preferred, or at least conventional, way of solving crimes, punishing evil, and dealing with problems. Mayhem caused by car chases is generally viewed as fun and games.

Prothrow-Stith calls for a movement "like that fueling the anti-smoking and drunk-driving campaigns.... Television and movies should portray the pain and suffering, the bad outcomes of violence."

She also calls on her medical colleagues to join in violence-prevention efforts. "Doctors cannot continue to stitch up the wounds and send that person back out on the street without addressing the problem," she says. "Violence can be reduced if America treats it as a public health emergency." But, she adds, "while working for such a change in professional and national attitudes, parents and educators must focus on taking action at home and in the schools."

To regard violent behavior in young people as a phase of normal development is wishful thinking. Almost every parent has listened to a child's complaints about the class bully whose antisocial behavior often includes extortion and threats to personal safety. Bullies usually pick on smaller, relatively defenseless, classmates. Should this be shrugged off as just a childish form of acting-out? In fact, the class bully may be on the way to terrorizing neighborhoods, and early intervention often can forestall more serious trouble later.

Noting the experiences of other countries is useful here. Japan has reported acute bullying problems in its schools, which have occasionally led to victims' suicides. Norway, one of the countries that has taken seriously the problem of bullying, has initiated an intervention program in forty-two schools. It has produced training materials for teachers, an information folder for parents, and videocassettes that show episodes from the everyday lives of two children who have been victims of bullying.

Interventions to eliminate bullying include making all students aware of the problem, actively involving teachers and parents in its prevention, setting firm limits against unacceptable behavior, and protecting potential victims. As a result of the Norwegian program, the incidents of bullying dropped by more than 50 percent in a two-year period. At the same time, antisocial behavior that is often related to bullying, such as theft, vandalism, and truancy, also declined significantly. Students reported that they were happier in their school life.

Dan Olweus, professor in the Department of Psychosocial Science at the University of Bergen, Norway, who conducted extensive studies of bullying in Norway and Sweden, said: "A student is bullied when he or she is exposed, repeatedly and over time, to negative actions of some kind from one or several students." At this point, adults must step in and punish the bully. "Bullying is part of a more general anti-social behavior pattern," Olweus said. "When we follow the former school bullies to age twenty-three, we find a four-fold increase in criminal behavior."

Some years ago, a highly successful teacher at a center for youngsters with serious emotional problems placed at the rear of his classroom a stereo with earphones on one side and a punching bag at the other. His instructions to the boys (in an all-male setting) was that whenever one of them felt restless or angry, he could get up, go to the back of the room, and either listen to some music or hit the punching bag. The boys took advantage of the offer. Disruptive behavior during and after class virtually ceased.

Such a traditional let-it-out approach continues to be an essential component in the prevention of adolescent violence. Physical activity provides an outlet for pent-up tensions, stress, and anger. The National School Safety Center points out that educators have long known that sports can serve as an antidote to delinquency and violence. An important caution, however, is that participation in sports and athletics must be open to *all* youngsters, not only to members of the schools' varsity teams.

Beyond the schools, recreational opportunities are provided by such organizations as the Police Athletic League, various boys' and girls' clubs, the scouts, and YMCAs and YWCAs. (See chapter 7 and Appendix.)

Despite the controversy over gun control, or perhaps because of it, any effort at preventing—or at least reducing—the threat of violence must come to grips with the issues of guns as a major adolescent health problem. While firearms are only part of the problem of violence, they are the tools most likely to make violent action fatal. Once a gun is available, conflict and anger become a threat to life and limb.

At a time when those who want to prevent violence urge a curb on the proliferation of firearms, it may nevertheless be necessary, if only as an interim measure, to include education in the safe use of guns. The nonprofit Center to Prevent Handgun Violence tries to educate the public about the dangers of careless use of firearms. Its message is that even having a licensed gun, in the home or on the person, is dangerous, and that it does not afford its owners the protection they seek. Being realistic, however, the center goes beyond such warnings. For example, it helped the Baltimore County Police Department develop an education program that teaches handgun owners to use and store their weapons safely, and particularly to "childproof" their weapons.

The Youth Advisory Council of the Detroit City Council, in conjunction with the Educational Fund to End Handgun Violence, in 1988 launched a special campaign directed at young people. One of its graphic posters, showing a morgue, was captioned: "Let's be honest. Not all kids who carry guns go to jail."

The United States has more gun control laws than any other nation in the world; there are literally thousands of federal, state, and local laws dealing with the sale, distribution, type, possession, and use of firearms. Yet, we suffer from a greater proliferation of guns and more widespread and deadly use of them than any other Western country. By now, it is evident that the existing gun control laws are far from effective and that the opponents of gun control are hard at work maintaining that dangerous status quo.

Until there is effective legislation, schools must do what they can to keep the weapons out. New York City, where 1,500 to 2,000 weapons are confiscated every year, has experimented with hand-held metal detectors used for random searches by security guards in the corridors of sixteen high schools. (Metal detectors like the ones used at airports were thought to be impractical because they slow down the entry of thousands of students at the start of each day.) Initial reports about the program's results are encouraging; they include statements from many students who said the use of the detectors has helped them feel more secure.

Not all educators agree. The Los Angeles school system, despite a growing weapons problem, rejected the use of metal detectors, partly, administrators say, because the buildings are used beyond school hours and in the evenings, making it easy to circumvent the detectors and to smuggle firearms into school buildings. Other opponents fear that the detectors send a negative message to the public about the schools. While many such critics prefer preventive measures that rely on human rather than technological safeguards, it seems clear that a comprehensive campaign must include both.

One personal approach is through peer education and mentoring—relying on respected older students to get young adolescents to understand the risks entailed in violence, particularly in the use of weapons. The most promising such programs now in use are those related to health education, such as Teens on Target (TNT), which emerged from the Oakland Safety Task Force in California, a coalition of parents, elected officials, and representatives of the schools and community agencies. TNT was created in 1988 after two shootings of junior high school students. A group of high school students selected from different racial and ethnic backgrounds were enlisted as paid violence-prevention advocates. The program deliberately involved young people as advocates on the assumption that they would be more effective in reaching young adolescents. They receive special training in a summer course designed to give them leadership and public speaking skills and to familiarize them with problems with drugs, alcohol, and guns.

Early results were gratifying. Once empowered as leaders in the antiviolence action, these advocates believed that they could be important actors in improving the world in which they lived. They acted as peer educators in high schools and as mentors to younger students in elementary and middle schools. One outcome was a joint neighborhood-school project aimed at establishing a gun- and drug-free zone in and around the schools. Publicity in the media followed.

TNT is planning to expand into other cities, but it is still too soon to form a firm judgment of its effectiveness. The program has not been without problems. Since it operates mainly in high-risk areas where there is an unfortunate turnover of school teaching staff, TNT members must constantly adjust to new participants whose experience and perspectives are not necessarily in tune with the program.

Traditionally, school administrators have often relied on suspension and expulsion in their efforts to be rid of unruly and disruptive students. The impulse to exclude such students is understandable, both for the administrators' peace of mind and in the interest of students whose chance to learn is being jeopardized. Yet, the suspension-expulsion tactic ultimately falls short of effectively addressing the crisis and may even perpetuate them in the long term. Suspended students return to class academically further behind their classmates, and they often express their frustration by becoming doubly disruptive. They are also more likely to drop out of school altogether. Expelling troublemakers may make the classroom more peaceful, but the expelled student is now on the streets as a potential threat to the community and often returns as an unwelcome intruder to a school that has rejected him.

Referring to the crisis proportions of adolescent violence, David Hamburg noted:

There is some kind of wild, even crazy, discrepancy between the high level of public concern and the lack of an organized constituency or a major thrust on the part of the funding agencies, and a very marginal, hands-off involvement of the universities and research institutes, as if this were some kind of low-brow activity. . . . Violence is not usually isolated from other aspects of a damaging way of life. And so violence and related problems have to be thought of together in terms of generic interventions to make differences in the lives of kids. . . .

I do hear from time to time . . . "Well, you know, some day, when we know more, we'll be able to intervene efficiently and at a lower cost, and let's wait for that day." But we simply have to ask, how much preventable damage is going to occur in that length of time? . . . You can let the perfect become the enemy of the good. . . . The right question to ask is, "Can we do better than we are doing now?"

Urgency is of the highest order. The deaths of children and adolescents are mounting every day, as are those of innocent victims caught in the crossfire. Beyond the deaths and the injuries there are the fears, the permanent psychological damage, the hidden hostilities that foster and feed violence, and the ultimate threat to civic peace and a free society. All of us are victims in that crossfire.

Violence undermines everything that should provide security to young people. The damage violence causes to adolescents' mental health, as well as their physical well-being, is immeasurable; it is always accompanied by unhealthy anger and fear, which severely stunt psychological growth.

Violence erodes and destroys all the relationships that are so vital to favorable adolescent development—between parents and children, between teachers and students, between peers, between young people and the future. To reduce violence in our homes, on our streets, in our schools is a task that must begin now.

CHAPTER SIX

IMAGE AND COMPETITION

VS.

NUTRITION AND EXERCISE

Every year the average young adolescent is exposed to at least 10,000 television commercials advertising food—most of it harmful to his or her health. This is particularly deplorable because it follows years of progress in America's nutritional habits in general.

"This century has seen a marked improvement in the health of American adolescents, but currently the trend is being reversed: Today's teenagers are in poorer health than their parents were at the same age. Mortality is mostly related to crime, drugs, and suicide, but there are also nonfatal health problems which have immediate and long-term consequences that require the attention and financial support of our society. Good nutrition and adequate physical activity must be recognized as a cost-effective means for normal growth and development during adolescence and for decreased risk of future chronic diseases."

The above statement is the introduction to a report on *Nutrition and Exercise: Effects on Adolescent Health,* by Carol N. Meredith and Johanna T. Dwyer of the School of Medicine at the University of California, Davis, and Tufts University Medical School in Boston. The authors continue: "In the past, undernutrition and overwork in unsanitary environments stunted the growth of many American children. Today, inadequate nutrition ranges from excesses that lead to obesity, to deficits that produce anemia or low-weight babies born to teenagers. At the same time, physical exercise paradoxically has become a 'leisure activity' that is more accessible to the rich than to the poor."

These concerns also extend to the accessibility of nutritious food. For the majority of Americans, more of every kind of nutritious food is constantly and conveniently available, while at the same time growing numbers of poor children and adolescents have deficient diets.

When it comes to eating properly and getting sufficient physical exercise, young Americans are aging in unhealthy ways. In general, the diets of adolescents today are less healthful than those of younger children. Also, during adolescence physical activity begins to decrease. Clearly, then, the way to achieve better health in future adult Americans is to establish and sustain healthier habits in adolescence. Fortunately, adult America has, in recent years, been paying much more attention to the risks of an unhealthy diet. The alert about the dangers of the intake of excessive fat, sugar, and salt and about cholesterol has been heeded. It appears, too, that adolescents are quite well informed about what sort of food is healthy and what is not. Their knowledge, however, has not been translated into general practice. When asked to identify the barriers that keep them from healthful eating, adolescents cite lack of time and self-discipline and an indifferent sense of the consequences.

According to a 1988 report by the U.S. surgeon general, two out of three Americans who neither drink nor smoke may find their long-term health prospects shaped by what they eat more than by any other personal behavior. Excess and imbalance are the most serious problems. The U.S. departments of Health and Human Services and of Agriculture, in their *Dietary Guidelines for Americans*, recommend the following: eat a variety of foods; maintain a healthy weight; avoid a diet high in fat and cholesterol; and include enough vegetables (cauliflower, broccoli, and cabbage), fruits, and grain products as well as consume sugar in moderation. The recommendations stand in sharp contrast to the diets of most adolescents and adults.

While the need for most vitamins and minerals rises

markedly during adolescence, teenagers' diets are often short of iron, calcium, and vitamin A. Low calcium intake is particularly damaging to the future health of girls. Unfortunately, about a fourth of the energy intake of adolescents comes from foods that are *low* in protein, vitamins, and minerals, such as desserts, soft drinks, candy, cookies, pies, cakes, salad dressings, and french fries and other deep-fried foods.

About 5 percent of adolescents skip meals regularly, and the omission of certain meals, such as breakfast, not only affects the total nutritional balance but also leads to an unhealthy reliance on nonnutritional snacks.

Extremes are always a problem: most adults now recognize that neither overweight nor excessive dieting is healthy. Today, about 26 percent of the population is overweight. The problem is particularly serious among the poor and some minorities. Obesity has been linked to increased risk of diabetes mellitus, high blood pressure and stroke, coronary heart disease, gallbladder disease, and some types of cancer. It is estimated that about 30 percent of all cancers are diet related. To prevent cancer, James F. Sallis of the Department of Pediatrics at the University of California, San Diego, recommends decreasing calories and fat and increasing vitamin A and vegetables.

Why worry about overweight in adolescents? Because overweight in the teenage years can persist in adulthood, especially if it already existed in childhood. Obese adolescents who are poor, or who are black, Mexican-American, and American Indian may be particularly likely to remain obese as adults. During and after adolescence, girls from poor families often become heavier than those from more affluent homes. Obese and sedentary parents often raise obese and sedentary children, while lean and active parents appear to transmit those qualities to their children.

Obese adolescents frequently are under psychological stress and often suffer from high blood pressure and high insulin levels, which can be predictors of health problems later on. Meredith and Dwyer warn in the 1991 *Annual Review of Public Health*: "Overt disease may be present in obese adolescents, but the risk of future health problems must be addressed by health educators and counselors, especially if family members are obese. Obesity that persists throughout childhood and adolescence is likely to be associated with increased risks of later hypertension, high serum cholesterol and coronary artery disease, adult onset of diabetes, gall bladder disease, certain forms of hormone-dependent cancer, and other medical problems.... Adolescents tend to consume too many calories and fats, too much sodium, and too little potassium, calcium, and iron."

Iris F. Litt, professor of pediatrics and director of Adolescent Medicine at Children's Hospital at Stanford University, warns that early puberty is a crucial time for the building of bone density through an adequate intake of calcium. On a positive note, she points out that nonfat yogurt, including frozen yogurt, both among adolescents' favored foods, are high in calcium content. (She also includes pizza, another teenage favorite, among the list of permissible foods.)

Just as obesity is dangerous, an overemphasis on being thin may cause such eating disorders as anorexia nervosa, a relentless, and sometimes fatal, obsession to become thinner that afflicts mainly girls, who represent about 95 percent of all anorexia cases. Bulimia (episodes of binge eating followed by self-induced vomiting and other forms of purging) also poses a special threat to adolescent girls. These eating disorders can produce severe clinical complications that may require hospitalization, especially in the case of anorexia. Treatment is difficult and involves the cooperation of psychiatrists, nutritionists, counselors, family therapists, and the adolescent's parents.

The *Woman's Guide to Stanford* quotes a student in her senior year: "I became a bulimic in high school, but as with most women with eating disorders, I started dieting seriously when I hit adolescence at around thirteen.... For incentive to lose weight, we competed against each other. We actually wrote up lists of taboo foods and signed our names at the bottom.... By age ten, and I know that I am not alone here either, various forces had successfully taught me to be afraid of food and to treat my body as an object whose needs I had to struggle against."

Lorraine L. Morgan, a director in Stanford's Program in Human Biology, has been counseling students in a coed dormitory of ninety-five residents. She is alarmed by the high number of eating disorders among the female students. For most of them, she says, the problem started at age ten or even earlier. An awareness of their mothers' extreme dieting was one factor these young people shared, she said. And as they grew older, many were impressed by hearing stories of long-married men "exchanging wives for younger, slimmer women." In a documentary film, *The Famine Within*, Katherine Gilday reports: "The average 5-foot-8-inch Miss America contestant weighed 132 pounds in 1954 and 117 pounds in 1980. . . . "

Recent studies show that almost 70 percent of young adolescent girls attempted to lose weight following the common weight gain that is the natural outcome of female development soon after puberty. A look at magazines that young girls read provides part of the answer: most of the models and starlets—the young women thought to symbolize sexual attraction—are pencil slim, implying that the thin figure catches the most desirable boys.

Young women with eating disorders are often depressed or under stress and suffer from low self-esteem. When looking in a mirror, anorexics who virtually starve themselves fail to see their emaciated bodies—they see instead a "mental" image of themselves as too fat. Litt notes that reaching the parents of young children is crucial in establishing positive attitudes toward eating and drinking.

Morgan called the prevalence of eating disorders among adolescents and young women "a health crisis." Other experts point out that adolescents with eating disorders also frequently use alcohol and drugs. The *American Journal of Public Health* reported in 1987 that female purgers showed higher rates of drunkenness and greater levels of psychological distress than their nonbulimic counterparts.

Girls who mature early are more likely to resort to extreme

dieting. The peak age for the onset of eating disorders is about fifteen to nineteen years. Many victims are white, middle or upper-middle class, well educated, attractive, and are of average or slightly below-average weight; but Litt points out that anorexia and bulimia occur in all ethnic groups, with the general exception of blacks, and that one-fourth of anorexic adolescents have little education and include some children of migrant farm workers. Litt considers sixth grade already too late to take preventive measures. "Eight years is not uncommon for self-induced vomiting," she says.

In a 1989 survey by Louis Harris Associates, 32 percent of elementary school youngsters said "yes" when asked if they have ever been on a diet. The proportions rose to 42 percent and 48 percent, respectively, in junior high and high school. Thirty-nine percent of the elementary school children and 55 percent of junior high school students said they dieted to look better rather than for health reasons.

Although adolescent boys are more likely to control their weight by exercising rather than dieting, a disturbing trend has recently arisen—mainly among adolescent boys: the use of anabolic steroids. Because this has become a serious problem among highly visible and respected adult athletes, it has influenced many adolescents. Steroids are used to induce a muscular physique thought to represent virility in addition to athletic prowess. By current estimates, 13 percent of high school athletes use steroids.

Because physical exercise can be carried to a health-threatening extreme, the most sensible way of dealing with adolescent weight-related health is to stress a balance between physical activity and a sensible diet.

This sounds easier than it is. Anyone who has observed teenagers' eating knows that nothing is more attractive than hamburgers and french fries, potato chips, ice cream, and a wide array of junk food. One survey of a nationally representative sample of eighth- and tenth-graders by the U.S. Public Health Service showed that 48 percent of the girls and 32 percent of the boys had not eaten breakfast on five or more days during the preceding week. On an average, students reported eating three snacks a day. More than half of those snacks were high in fat and/or sugar. Nearly four out of every ten students had eaten fried foods four or more times a week.

As already noted, television plays a highly negative role in shaping the diets of young people. Many of its commercials promote high-sugar-content cereals, candy, gum, and cookies and high-fat hamburgers. Products without sugar content appear in fewer than 5 percent of the ads, and vegetables are hardly ever advertised. "This barrage of messages to eat unhealthy foods is designed to be appealing to youth; is produced and broadcast at great expense; and is repeated many times every day, so the influence of TV must be considered in planning comprehensive dietary promotion intervention," notes Sallis. "Television viewing is correlated with between-meal snacking, consumption of the types of food advertised on TV, and attempts to influence the food purchases by mother."

Responsible critics have been vocal but, unfortunately, with few results. In July 1991, the American Academy of Pediatrics called for a ban on food commercials aimed at children, asserting that such advertising only promotes profits for the advertiser without concern for the health and well-being of young consumers. Earlier in the year, the Center for Science in the Public Interest charged that in the program period for children, often referred to as the "cartoon ghetto," 96 percent of the Saturday morning food advertisements were sugary cereals, candy, cookies, and junk food.

Extended television watching also cuts into time for physical activity. Studies show that for youngsters who watch less than one hour of television a day, only 10 percent are obese, compared with 20 percent for those who watch television five hours or more.

The lure of unhealthy food is everywhere. Sallis observes: "The availability of the amount and variety of food that characterizes American society is probably unprecedented in the history of humankind. . . . There is food at home. There are stores and vending machines at school. Every time a teen gets in a car, rides a bike to a friend's house, or walks down the street, those streets are seemingly lined with convenience stores.... Health promotion programs will have to be extremely powerful if the successful marketing practices of the food industry are to be countered."

Where should these programs begin?

REALISTIC INCENTIVES FOR NUTRITION

As with all admonitions to teenagers against habits that put their health and safety at risk, warning them about the consequences of poor eating habits hardly produces either compliance or concern. How many teenagers are likely to take seriously nutritional prescriptions whose benefits may not be realized until forty years later? The promise of instant gratification does not readily give way to an investment in good health that far down the road. The threat of early osteoporosis as a result of calcium deficiency, for example, seems quaint to a twelve-year-old. As noted earlier, one way to overcome such obstacles is to combine education regarding sensible nutrition with broader concerns about protecting the environment, an issue about which many adolescents have very strong feelings.

Fortunately, a healthy diet can also be tasty. Encouraging, too, is the current interest in athletics that prevails among so many young girls: their growing interest in having stronger and more muscular bodies offers some hope that there may be a gradual decline in their obsession with thinness.

The schools are the best place for preventive and remedial action because that is where most youngsters can be reached. Most secondary schools provide some health education classes that address issues of nutrition and physical exercise. However, they are usually offered in no more than five or six sessions— not nearly enough to counteract all the contrary messages that promote unhealthy diets and other poor eating habits.

Much of the instruction also comes too late. Young adolescents should learn well before the fact that weight gain at puberty is natural and necessary. (See chapter 2.) This is the time to reassure young girls and to prevent them from panicking at the changes that will take place in their bodies. The proper time to start weaving food-related messages into the curriculum, Litt recommends, is at age six.

To develop healthy behavior, a few successful school lunch programs serve whole-grain bread and fresh fruit alongside salad bars—but these are the exceptions. It is ironic that too many schools themselves cater to youngsters' unhealthy food preferences and thereby encourage poor nutrition. In many schools, too, students find it easy to avoid the relatively healthier cafeteria offerings by getting snacks out of vending machines, which are either within the school or in nearby fast-food stores.

One generally overlooked problem in school cafeterias, says Litt, is the reluctance of some teenage girls to eat at all in the presence of boys, apparently because they feel that the very act of eating is unattractive.

However, some progress should be acknowledged. In response to growing criticism, fast-food dispensers have begun to produce and to advertise some healthier, or at least less health-damaging, products, and the Food and Drug Administration is clamping down on misleading labeling. These trends deserve support.

In addition to early education in proper nutrition, teenagers should be given incentives to be wise and discriminating consumers. They need to acquire the judgment to become sensitive to seductive advertising and the ability to resist its lure when shopping in supermarkets and eating in fast-food restaurants.

The problem of faulty diet and lack of exercise may be compounded for youngsters growing up in poor neighborhoods where frequently shops do not stock a selection of low-fat and low-salt foods. Exercise is difficult to come by in such areas where public recreation facilities, such as parks and playgrounds, are scarce and streets are too dangerous for jogging or other outdoor exercise.

As with most adolescent behavior, peer influence is crucial in promoting healthy nutrition, but adult professionals must also play a constructive role. Primary-care physicians, for example, should routinely counsel their adolescent patients on what is a desirable diet and what is adequate and appropriate exercise. Physicians who conduct sports-related examinations should take the time to caution young people against excessive exertion, extreme dietary practices, and the use of steroids.

IMPROVED OPPORTUNITY FOR EXERCISE

In the United States, an estimated 35 million children and youths between the ages of six and eighteen participate in one or more organized sports every year. That such numbers of young people engage in physical exercise is encouraging, but serious gaps remain: too little organized sport is offered to poor and minority youngsters and to girls. In addition, young athletes often do not eat the proper quantity of food required for sound nutrition. Anxious to appear lean and to "fit" into a specific weight classification, many adolescents reduce their food intake to the point of undernourishment. Among girls, the problem tends to be more pronounced among dancers, gymnasts, skaters, and runners.

Young people of both genders sometimes employ dehydration to reduce their weight, through excessive sweating, limited fluid intake, and the use of diuretics. Repeated dehydration and rehydration can be harmful to the kidneys.

School systems should provide daily physical education classes for all students. Until recently, most school coaches were teachers in their schools, but as teachers grow older, and as communities increase their pressure on schools to produce winning teams, teachers have become less able and less willing to take on coaching tasks. More and more coaches are hired from outside the education world, and they are far more likely than their "teacher" predecessors to bend to community preoccupation with "winning."

The nationwide reduction in public school funding has created grave problems in low-income areas, including the loss of such extracurricular activities as sports and athletics. In contrast, sports programs for affluent families are increasingly conducted on a "for-profit" basis, in gymnastics, swimming, track, tennis, and skating clubs. The training in such clubs is often intense, sometimes requiring children to practice twelve to thirty hours a week. The social life of these children is often linked to that of other club members, leaving little time for normal activities with other children of their age.

Unfortunately, many youngsters are not introduced to sports until they enter junior high school, where their abilities are likely to be on public display, at the very age when they are most self-conscious, fearful, and easily embarrassed. The dread of public ridicule causes many youngsters to drop out of athletic activities.

School officials should be sensitive to the dangers of overemphasizing the importance of varsity team sports to the detriment of noncompetitive sports and having fun while also getting healthy exercise. Frequently overlooked is the fact that participation in most school and college varsity sports fails to carry over into adult life. Teenagers who concentrate on such team sports as football, baseball, and basketball tend, later in life, to trade off their physical activity for the sedentary "pursuit" of watching games on television. It is in early adolescence that the foundation must be built for youngsters to want to continue with active sports and exercise in their adult lives—and not in terms of competition, but with an emphasis on good health and well-being.

Yet, competition for victory is still the order of the day. While physical education, primarily in the form of team sports, attracts a great deal of public attention, almost half of high school seniors do not participate in it.

These concerns also apply to many community organizations involved in sports and physical health activity. An unhealthy preoccupation with winning often begins at a very early age for the many youngsters who engage in Little League games. A distorted drive to win and the shame of losing causes many young athletes to become disappointed and frustrated and to give up because they failed to measure up to misguided adult standards for achievement.

Coaches should do everything possible to promote their players' self-confidence. Research has shown that one way to enhance the self-esteem of nine- to twelve-year-olds is by following up a player's error with a combination of supportive coaching and encouragement. The success of such an approach is illustrated by a study of teams who were coached by people trained in offering good support: 95 percent of the youngsters returned to play the following year, whereas only 75 percent of players guided by untrained coaches came back for more.

As adolescents, particularly in the suburbs, get driver's licenses, their time spent walking or bicycling declines. It is estimated that spontaneous physical activity decreases by about 50 percent between the ages of twelve and eighteen. Participation in physical education classes declines from about 98 percent of the school enrollment at age ten to 50 percent at age seventeen. Participation in all physical exercise peaks at age ten. The rate then steadily declines until age fourteen, at which point there is a sharp drop, according to a Youth Sports Institute report.

Ironically, part of the reason for the decline is the start of interscholastic competition, which eliminates half of the young people who participated earlier but who cannot qualify in the newly competitive enterprise. Other reasons teenagers cite for dropping out of sports activities are "not having much fun," "practice is boring," and "sports take up too much time."

Deeply embedded prejudices have long cheated girls of the benefits of athletics and sports. Just as male domination had closed most professions to women until well into the twentieth century, so it was argued that sports can be harmful to women; sports might damage women's reproductive organs and cause them to develop muscles that are unattractive. Other long-held myths claimed that women lack the self-confidence and toughness needed to compete successfully in sports. The persisting male opposition to giving women equal access to sports was bluntly expressed by Bill Knepper, a pitcher for the Houston Astros: "I don't think women were created by God to be a physical, hard person. I think God created women to be feminine."

All this is reminiscent of a time when it was accepted medical opinion that ovaries and the brain could not develop at the same time. In 1879, William Goodell wrote approvingly in *Lessons in Gynecology*: "Our great-grandmothers . . . knew less about Euclid and the classics than they did about housekeeping and housework. But they made good wives and mothers, and bore and nursed sturdy sons and buxom daughters and plenty of them at that."

Since the enactment of federal Title IX legislation mandating equal opportunity in school and college athletics, girls' participation in sports has increased. In girls' interscholastic high school sports, the increase is dramatic—from 300,000 in 1970 to 1.8 million in 1984. (The change in attitudes is also reflected on the Olympic level: in summer Olympics, women competitors rose from zero in 1896 to 2,476 in 1988.) Nevertheless, males are still favored and will continue to be as long as men dominate in the management of sports.

Debunking the myths about girls' inferior capacity to engage in sports—a myth that is clearly a threat to their healthy development—is a task for parents, physical education teachers, youth sports coaches, researchers, journalists, and all those who set policies in sports. The goal must be to acknowledge that sports is a health-enhancing *human* activity. This calls for an early start: it is during childhood that competence in motor skills is developed by throwing, catching, jumping, hopping, and skipping. By age six, children can use these skills to create games. Unfortunately, many parents respond differently to boys and girls in encouraging the development of these skills. When teenage girls show competence in certain sports, for example, they are often told, disparagingly, "You play like a boy."

The fact that poor youngsters often have limited access to organized physical activity has been well documented, and serious obstacles remain to full-scale participation of minorities in some sports. In particular, greater efforts must be made at every public and private level to hire minority men and women as coaches to act as role models.

At the same time, the crucial part that academic success in school plays in healthy adolescent development is too often ignored in encouraging budding athletes. Telling young black and Hispanic adolescents that achievement in athletics alone can pave the road to economic security places their futures at serious risk. Coaches and teachers must recognize that even the most promising young athletes need to understand that they are gambling their future livelihood on very limited opportunities if they neglect their studies.

The obvious benefits of sports should not obscure the many real risks of injury. Some such risks are inevitable, but most sports-related injuries can be prevented by proper supervision, careful conditioning, well-functioning protective equipment, and attention to safety. Preventing injuries is an essential part of promoting health. Young people who are about to participate in sports programs should first receive physical examinations. Even minor injuries must be properly treated to prevent them from turning into potentially chronic health problems.

One way to prevent injuries is for coaches and trainers to be sensitive to the difference between chronological and biological age in young people's development. A group of thirteen-year-olds may include some boys and girls whose biological development endows them with size and strength equivalent to that of sixteen-year-olds or, at the other end of the scale, the equivalent of ten-year-olds. These physical differences are significant, especially in contact sports such as football. If coaches ignore these differences, they needlessly expose more slowly maturing adolescents to failure and humiliation within the group or team and to serious injury that could threaten their health in adulthood.

Responsible supervisors also should teach youngsters the importance of avoiding injuries caused by excessive exercise, such as engaging in endurance running, pitching, or tennis-ball serving and other such activities that are beyond the tolerance of adolescent muscle structure. The Youth Sports Institute cites as a model adolescent sports program Dixie Baseball Incorporated, which provides oversight and administration of youth baseball and softball for approximately 320,000 youngsters in eleven southern states. While a fee is charged for participation, no one is excluded because of inability to pay.

Another model approach is a "coach effectiveness training program" based in Seattle. Youth coaches are taught how to avoid punishing and criticizing their young players and to develop positive relationships among team members. As a result, the young players reported that they liked each other more and had more fun in the games. Most encouraging, young people who started out with low self-esteem became more confident.

A "Physical Education At-Risk Youth Program," which was inaugurated by faculty members at the University of Chicago, concentrates on the most deprived minority youngsters. It stresses social, emotional, and spiritual health in conjunction with physical health. Instead of focusing on winning, it aims at leading youngsters toward caring and helping each other, practicing self-control, and setting realistic personal goals.

The Hawaii Youth Sports and Physical Fitness Program, established in 1989 by the Hawaii State Legislature, has already educated 6,000 coaches who recruit children and adolescents for participation in organized sports. About half of the children come from low socioeconomic backgrounds. The program's directors check on the youngsters' physical fitness, inform their parents and the young athletes themselves about proper nutrition, and also counsel them on the dangers of drugs.

The combination of sound nutrition and proper physical exercise is crucial to adolescent health, not only for today, but for young people's long-term future.

CHAPTER SEVEN

PROGRAMS FOR YOUNG PEOPLE

THE YOUTH ORGANIZATION

AS FAMILY SUPPLEMENT

The director of a local youth organization tells a visiting political leader: "You should know about Darlene—and, oh yes, her brother, Tyrone, too. But we call him Toot around here. [Their] mother died of AIDS six months ago. [Their] father left them and two younger girls. Darlene brings the younger ones to the Girls Club at 7:00 each morning, and we send them off to school and then keep them occupied while she's at work after school. Toot works all day and picks the girls up at 7:00 each night, after he leaves the Boys Club, where he boxes. He feeds the girls and gets them to bed before Darlene gets home. Each day it's the same."

This brief vignette appeared in the April 1991 issue of the *Phi Delta Kappan* in an article entitled "Community Organizations as Family." It is excerpted from research on constructive adolescent activities by Shirley Brice Heath, professor of English, and Milbrey Wallin McLaughlin, professor of education, both at Stanford University.

While the excerpt highlights an extreme case, it is a telling example of the changing world of families and the concurrent changes and vital new roles being taken on by youth organizations. These organizations continue their more traditional roles as well: to serve youngsters as social and recreational centers for fun, relaxation, and physical fitness. But increasingly, they are assuming a crucial new role for children and youths at high risk, and that new role is to supplement incomplete or inadequate families and families who are simply too poor to provide for their children's needs. Two issues have created additional and equally serious responsibilities for youth organizations: the need to give young adolescents insight into their own sexuality and the necessity for education about how to protect themselves from the dangers of sexually transmitted diseases, especially AIDS.

A 1986 Minneapolis study found that 30 to 40 percent of ten- to twelve-year-olds return from school to homes without the presence of adults between three and five days a week. Boys are more likely than girls to be left unsupervised, and African-American boys are most often left unsupervised. This situation is certainly not what parents want, and African-American families are even more likely than white families to believe that their children need supervision. For example, more than twice as many white parents (26 percent) as African-American parents (11 percent) think that their children can safely manage on their own at age twelve. With decreased government spending, youngsters who need supervision most are least likely to get it. The Minneapolis study showed that urban minority youngsters between the ages of ten and twelve who live in one-parent homes are less frequently (44 percent) involved in after-school programs than are their suburban counterparts (63 percent).

Concern about this extends to young people of all ages. Fern Marx of the Wellesley College Center for Research on Women notes in a report for the Children's Defense Fund: "Traditionally, attention to the problems of latch-key children has been focused on the supervision of elementary school children before and after school and on days the schools are closed. Yet, there is a growing consensus that young adolescents between the ages of ten and fifteen may also be at risk when left on a regular basis in unsupervised settings."

Parents of young teens are increasingly fearful that if their children are not engaged in supervised activities they will be more likely to engage in delinquent behavior or become victims or perpetrators of crime. Many parents who are at work and, therefore, absent from home worry that bad influences may propel their children toward drinking, drug abuse, theft, fights, and involvement with gangs. They consider unsupervised neighborhood play neither safe nor constructive, and they are fearful that their children may be exposed not only to injury from accidents but to physical, sexual, or psychological abuse by older youths or adults.

These concerns were found to be fairly uniform among parents regardless of socioeconomic status. Even when the dangers are less alarming, parents worry about their unsupervised children's boredom, excessive time spent on the telephone, consumption of nonnutritious snacks, and too many hours spent watching television.

Parents' concerns about their children's sexual activity are well founded. A recent study showed that 20 percent of young adolescents engaged in sexual activity in their own homes when left alone and that 40 percent of teenagers from single-parent families were sexually active while the parent was absent. The increase in AIDS and other sexually transmitted diseases and in unwanted pregnancies underscores the need for constructive, supervised after-school activities and for the ability of youth organizations to attract and engage this vulnerable age group.

NO LONGER A LUXURY

What is obvious today is that youth organizations are no longer a luxury. Without them, large numbers of adolescents could fall into the traps of dangerous and harmful behavior. Thousands more would seek companionship, thrills, and power by joining youth gangs or would resort to fighting loneliness and depression by the use of alcohol and drugs.

As Jane Quinn, director of the Project on Youth Development and Community Programs of the Carnegie Council on Adolescent Development, points out, youth organizations rank second only to public schools in the number of young people they serve. Sociologist Judith Erickson, author of the *Directory of American Youth Organizations*, estimates that there are more than 400 national youth organizations. The fifteen largest (including Girl Scouts, Boy Scouts, Boys and Girls Clubs, Camp Fire, 4-H Clubs, Girls Incorporated, the YWCA, and the YMCA) serve approximately 30 million young people per year. Similar services are provided by a vast network of religious youth groups, sports and recreation programs, grass-roots community organizations, and programs supported by museums and libraries.

Most youth organizations consider health promotion to be one of their major functions, and an increasing number include education about substance abuse, sexuality, and AIDS prevention as part of their programming.

Of the leading national youth organizations (see Appendix), the largest is 4-H, with nearly 5 million participants. The smallest are ASPIRA, the only national Hispanic youth organization that provides intensive and successful educational enrichment programs to some 13,000 adolescents annually, and WAVE, Inc., a dropout-prevention and intervention program that serves some 8,000 teenagers each year. For the past twenty years, ASPIRA has operated a Health Careers Program to address the urgent need in the Hispanic community for medical and health-care practitioners. While Boys Scouts of America provides no statistics on its members' race, ethnicity, or family income, Boys and Girls Clubs of America reports that 51 percent of its membership consists of minorities, and 66 percent is classified as low income.

Although they are diverse in almost every aspect, the organizations nevertheless reflect certain common elements: a commitment to the effective development of young people; reliance on small-group activities under the guidance of committed adults; and the engagement of their participants in the process of cooperative learning.

Regardless of the size of the overall organization, effective youth programs recognize how important it is that members believe that they are part of an intimate group that creates a sense of belonging. "Successful organizations," the Heath and McLaughlin report notes, "adopt an approach that is both firm and flexible; they empower rather than infantilize youths; they are clear about their goals and their rules of membership." The report goes on to point out that Toot, who was mentioned earlier, learned to box while in the Boys Club and subsequently taught boxing to younger boys. Like many others, he came to value the organization as a fortress against an often unfriendly outside world. It was a place that was his; it offered him the elements of a safe and constructive life, the kind of life that a normal, healthy teenager could count on.

The rules of such successful organizations for young people are simple but crucial: do not hang out with gang members, do not use drugs or alcohol, and demonstrate a sense of responsibility as a representative of the group to the outside world.

Most organizations that offer programs to adolescents know that drug education and prevention deserve high priority; however, there is no consensus among them about how to succeed. For example, Quinn observes that Boy Scouts of America has chosen an approach that uses scare tactics, as illustrated by its prevention program, Drugs: A Deadly Game. Such an appeal is sharply criticized by many experts who favor a comprehensive approach that openly addresses the facts of drug use and offers concrete alternatives. Boys and Girls Clubs of America has developed the kind of research-based life skills and social competence approach through its Smart Moves program that is beginning to show encouraging results. (See chapter 3.)

The most effective leaders of youth organizations know that, in order to succeed, they must constantly ask themselves how best to appeal to the needs and wants of young adolescents. Surveys show that the two main attractions are fun and friends— not very different from what adults look for in the organizations and clubs they join. When the question is put to them, young adolescents say that they look for activities that are relevant to their lives, now and in the future, and they often mention issues of sexuality and career education as being of particular personal interest.

As noted throughout this book, young people today need to be taught life skills that help them cope with their vulnerable adolescent existence; they need a setting that makes it easy for them to talk with their peers and that also offers the support and advice of understanding adults; and they need a chance to make what they believe are useful contributions to their communities. The last is particularly important, because many undesirable and even dangerous actions by teenagers derive from their feeling of uselessness.

Usefulness implies competence, however, and the acquisition of competence has become a murky province indeed for millions of young people. The Life Skills Training working group of the Carnegie Council on Adolescent Development offers this comment on the issue: "Because of profound changes in our society over the past few decades, it can no longer be assumed that these skills are automatically learned. Contemporary adolescents need help in acquiring a range of social competencies, to cope with academics, to meet fundamental challenges of forming stable human relationships, to maintain hope about their future, to understand and adopt health-promoting behaviors, to make wise decisions about life options, and to optimize use of social networks."

Because youth organizations can contribute much to the development of healthy adolescents, they should be accessible to young people whose health and well-being are most at risk: the poor, who are also likely to be members of minorities. As Karen J. Pittman of the Academy for Educational Development's Center for Youth Development and Policy Research puts it in a paper prepared for the Council, "Given the real concerns about high-risk behaviors among youth . . . in high-risk environments, organizations in the voluntary sector should be assessed not only on their ability to make a good kid better, but to help those in trouble or at risk of being in trouble."

On this score, says Pittman, youth-serving organizations

have a mixed record. Some, working in high-risk areas, have made strong commitments to serving poor and minority youths. The majority of youngsters served by Girls Incorporated and Boys and Girls Clubs, for example, are members of minority groups. Other organizations serve predominantly white, advantaged populations. Most fall between these poles. All indications, however, point to the fact that youngsters at risk give high ratings to the programs offered by youth organizations, and there is encouraging evidence of the beneficial health-related impact of these programs on adolescents.

As demonstrated by the results of recent programs, Boys and Girls Clubs that operate in public housing projects were found to deal effectively with the most serious problems faced by adolescents living there, including drug use and early pregnancy.

Nevertheless, youth programs proliferate among those who need them least. In an analysis for the Carnegie Council, Elliott A. Medrich noted that, in general, both "the public and nonprofit sectors tend to concentrate their efforts on providing for those inclined to participate. The needs or interests of nonusers are rarely considered." In earlier studies, he has pointed to the significant disparity in the availability of nonschool services between upper- and lower-income neighborhoods. While this view appears to make a sharp distinction between the services provided by youth organizations to poor children and those from affluent homes, it is clear that a comprehensive regard for the needs and aspirations of all adolescents should lead to a fusion rather than a gap between the two.

What emerges from a thoughtful review is the simple truth that youth organization programs are important to the health of all young adolescents, regardless of their socioeconomic background. As already noted, for example, young people at every income level tend to become more sedentary as they grow older, and this poses new risks to their health. An illustration of an organization built around strenuous but exciting outdoor exertion is Outward Bound. Originally concentrated on exploration in rural areas, in woods, and on mountains, it has begun to function in inner cities where poor youngsters are in particular need of liberation from confinement in the streets. In each school that participates in a New York City Outward Bound program, students are enrolled in a class taught by a regular teacher and an Outward Bound instructor. After school and on weekends, the students, many of whom have never left the city, engage in backpacking expeditions, rock climbing, and outdoor community service activities. In class, they read and write about their field experiences.

In general, says Christen Smith, executive director of the American Association for Leisure and Recreation, adolescents between the ages of thirteen and sixteen tend to stop attending organized recreation programs. There is a feeling among these youngsters that youth programs are "too tame" or overly organized and, therefore, too much like school. This underscores what most of the research indicates: that it is important for organizers of youth programs to be sensitive to adolescent preferences and to respond to both their needs and their interests at the ages when they seek greater independence.

For all young adolescents, but especially for those who are growing up in poor neighborhoods, physical safety is a matter of daily, overriding concern. One important function of after-school programs is to provide such safety as a condition for enjoyable and useful activities. Milwaukee, for instance, found that evening programs for girls could succeed only if they were offered at a safe place located near the girls' homes.

Fern Marx lists four critical features to which organizers must be sensitive: children must find their friends in the program; the activities must be of immediate interest; the adults in charge must understand youngsters; and they must allow them a feeling of autonomy. To attract parents, organizers should be aware of somewhat different priorities: affordable cost, easy transportation, and a staff that demonstrates child-rearing values compatible with their own.

Heath and McLaughlin suggest, in a study funded by the

Spencer Foundation, that organizations working with inner-city teenagers could learn much from the gangs that are their "rivals" for adolescents' attention. Like gangs, successful youth organizations should have strong roots in the community. Among the most popular and effective neighborhood organizations were found to be a tumbling team that gives more than 650 performances a year and that has a waiting list of 3,000 prospective members; a basketball team that has mandatory homework sessions supervised by the coach; and an improvisational theater troupe that examines issues of sex, gangs, drugs, and AIDS in performances before its teen peers.

SECRETS OF SUCCESS

Successful organizations, the report says, view their young members as resources to be developed rather than as problems to be fixed. They see youngsters in a positive light and try to create a comfortable environment for them, providing both physical safety and emotional security. The goal is a family-like structure that fosters a sense of mutual support and loyalty. Like families, successful youth organizations are available to their members during days, nights, and weekends. They ask their members to be guided, not by a series of specific rules, but by a broad sense of behavior that flows from a shared philosophy and is taken seriously.

Smith cites L. A. BEST as an exemplary after-school program for youth in Los Angeles. It is offered at nineteen schools located in high-crime areas and provides education, recreation, nutrition, reading, homework assistance, tutoring, and experience with computers. The program includes field trips, performing arts presentations, instruction in science, music, and history, antigang and antidrug education, and athletic competitions.

Similar programs are offered in Milwaukee, Newark, Atlanta, and in growing numbers of other communities. No hard statistics currently exist about their success in reducing behavior that endangers adolescent health, but a 1990 report by the

Children's Defense Fund notes that youths who lack access to organized after-school activities are more susceptible to peer pressure and harmful and dangerous activity.

The Michigan Department of Public Health reported that negative adolescent activities actually serve as a form of recreation to satisfy the young person's need to seek thrills, excitement, glamour, and high-risk adventure. The challenge to youth organizations is clear: to provide a satisfying, constructive, and safe alternative. One unusual example is in Montgomery County, Maryland. Its midnight basketball league captures the attention and engages the energies of adolescents during what are considered the high-risk hours.

Outreach is vital. Smith warns that at-risk young people may choose not to participate in organized community recreation programs for a number of reasons: they may not have the necessary social skills to fit easily into a group; recreation staff may lack the disposition and the training to work with them because they consider them "troublemakers" and discourage them from joining.

Girls, too, are often discouraged as a group from taking part in community programs, ostensibly because of concern for their safety. Because of society's stereotypes, many activities are regarded as too dangerous or strenuous for girls. Current research also shows that fewer resources are allocated to programs for girls. To remove these barriers, more women must be included in the planning of youth activities, and female staff members should serve as role models for the youngsters.

The great value of youth-service organizations, particularly after-school programs, is widely recognized by school officials. Thirty-seven percent of principals who responded to a poll by the National Association of Elementary School Principals in 1988 believed that children will do better in school if they are not left unsupervised during the time they spend outside school. But only 22 percent of the principals reported that they had before- or after-school programs in their school buildings, and 84 percent agreed that such programs are needed.

Alumni of youth-serving organizations report that they contributed significantly to their personal development. Eighty-one percent of Girl Scouts surveyed in a Louis Harris poll reported that their scouting experience was important to them. Six out of ten black Scouts and more than four out of ten Hispanic and American Indian girls found scouting of significant personal importance, as did one-third of whites and one-fourth of Asians. The highest praise came from girls living in large cities.

The respondents to a 1986 Louis Harris survey of alumni of Boys Clubs of America who had been members between 1920 and 1980 gave the organization high marks, considered that it contributed to their success in later years, and recalled that it provided a refuge from the streets and a support system against delinquency and drugs.

Among sixth- through twelfth-graders in single-parent homes, or in families with a history of abuse or parental addiction, the evidence shows that those who participated in religious organizations, extracurricular school activities, or community clubs and youth organizations were significantly less likely to engage in at-risk behavior.

In four consecutive annual evaluations, participants in the Teen Outreach Program (TOP) sponsored by the Junior Leagues International had, on average, a 16 percent lower rate of school suspensions, a 36 percent lower rate of school dropouts, and a 42 percent lower rate of pregnancies than youngsters in the control group who did not benefit from TOP membership.

A number of communities have youth programs that keep pace with the realistic needs and interests of their members. Smith cites as an example City Streets in Phoenix, which provides recreation activities for adolescents, most of them between the ages of twelve and sixteen. A youth council and a parent support group help in planning programs that offer sports tournaments, concerts, dances, talent shows, and field trips. Disc jockeys visit schools during lunch hour to play music and distribute information about their station's programs to attract young listeners.

Marx cites Plaza de La Raza, "a place for the people," a Los Angeles program that includes a community center, a park, a museum, a gallery, a theater, a gathering place for parents and young people, and a School for Performing and Visual Arts. Plaza de La Raza communicates Hispanic culture to the greater Los Angeles community while conducting classes in the arts for all age groups from elementary school to adulthood.

Other programs that are effective because they address the needs of their constituents include the West End Neighborhood House, Inc., in Wilmington, Delaware, a 101-year-old pioneer in the youth-service business. Today, one-third of the population it serves lives below the poverty level, and 40 percent of the young people's families are headed by a single parent. The goals of the program are "prevention, motivation, and stimulation." One of the program directors, who oversees four professionals, thirty volunteers, and ten peer workers who serve 1,100 low-income minority youngsters, says: "We want to prevent school dropouts, teenage pregnancy and problems with the law, but we also want to furnish some emotional stability and continuity so these kids can build a sense of self-worth." The center, which works with youngsters in academics, team sports, and various aspects of personal growth, is open from early afternoon until 9:00 P.M. during the school year, and from 8:00 A.M. to 9:00 P.M. during the summer months. Organizers say their aim is to create a participant-centered "home away from home."

One of the center's most popular programs for teenagers is a series of twice-weekly structured rap sessions on selected topics moderated by staff members. Additional services are health related, such as the administration of flu shots, cancer screening, prenatal programs, and other efforts aimed at preventing illness.

The Dorchester (Massachusetts) Youth Collaborative, founded in 1978, offers counseling and outreach to young people experiencing the ravages of poverty, social maladjustment, truancy, and repeated failure in schoolwork and community life. The organization tries to inform young people about available youth services and clubs. In 1982, the collaborative started an education program to provide tutoring, and a year later it inaugurated a crime prevention project.

The Girls Club of Dallas seeks to teach girls how to make the decisions that will affect their lives and to develop their talents. It provides a safe environment for youngsters who might otherwise be on the streets or who would return to empty homes after school. The club offers academic remediation and enrichment, sports and recreation, creative arts, crafts and dance, job counseling and training, and family life education, including pregnancy prevention.

The dire consequences of adolescent ignorance about sexuality have been ignored for many years on many levels of our society. (See chapter 3.) Membership surveys conducted by the YWCA and 4-H registered the urgent need for sex education over two decades ago. In 1981, the Congress of Camp Fire, Inc., gave almost unanimous approval to supplement families' responsibility by offering sex education, and other youth programs have worked in various ways to respond as well.

Girls Incorporated is considered a leader among national youth organizations in its commitment to providing family life and sexuality education to its members. The organization also has joined several national coalitions in promoting sexuality education and in assuring that adolescents have access to clinical services.

As noted earlier (see chapter 3), a three-year study conducted in 1991 by Girls Incorporated reported that teenage pregnancies could be reduced greatly by a comprehensive program that equips girls with communications skills and hope for a productive future as well as reproductive health services. The study was conducted among 750 girls between the ages of twelve and seventeen in Dallas, Memphis, Omaha, and Wilmington. Participation in the program reduced by half the proportion of girls aged twelve to fourteen who started to have sexual intercourse, and it also cut in half the number of pregnancies among those between the ages of fifteen and seventeen.

The study strongly suggests that such high-risk characteristics as dependence on welfare, living in an inner-city neighborhood in a fatherless household, and having mothers and friends who became pregnant as young teenagers need not predestine girls to become teenage mothers.

Corrian Spencer, eighteen, who participated in the program in Dallas and then went on to college told the *New York Times* (October 2, 1991): "I learned that I didn't have to go that way. I wanted to finish high school and have a different life for myself." She said she had founded a "virgins club" among her teenage friends.

Two of the Girls Incorporated program components are geared to young girls who have not yet become sexually active. Two other components are for girls who may already be sexually active but have not yet become pregnant.

In Growing Together, a program for the younger girls (ages nine to eleven), five two-hour mother-daughter workshops encourage communication about sexuality. Will Power/Won't Power, another program that is delivered in six two-hour sessions, offers assertiveness training to show youngsters (ages twelve to fourteen) that they can refuse sexual activity without losing friends.

A third component, for young women aged fifteen to eighteen, seeks to persuade participants that it is in their best interest to avoid pregnancy by focusing on educational and career plans, setting goals for themselves, and making sensible decisions about their lives.

A final component, Health Bridge, links teaching about sexuality with health and birth control services when appropriate.

Other organizations that address adolescent sexuality and teen pregnancy prevention include the American Red Cross, Boys and Girls Clubs of America, Girls Scouts of the U.S.A., the Salvation Army, and the Young Women's Christian Association.

Among the advantages of youth organizations offering family and sex education is the chance that parents will join in the support of such crucial teaching and that their participation will counteract misinformed opposition to providing teenagers with the information they so urgently need.

The AIDS epidemic has given the need for realistic sex education even greater urgency. The Carnegie Council's Jane Quinn points out that "the same factors that make youth agencies appropriate providers of sexuality education serve to make those settings effective in delivering AIDS education. . . . The adults who work with youth in such settings usually have established a high level of trust and possess good communication skills which enables members to feel comfortable exploring sexual issues with these leaders." These youth workers also have a good chance to inspire the trust of parents and other community members.

Youth organizations are also well placed to challenge the sense of immortality that is so common among young people. Quinn explains: "The hidden and long-term nature of the disease, coupled with young people's . . . feeling of invulnerability, combine forces to lead adolescents to conclude that 'it won't happen to me.' The hard-won credibility of the youth worker can serve to help convince young people of the very real threat of AIDS."

Like the schools, however, youth organizations are themselves vulnerable to becoming targets of controversy by opponents to sex education, who mistakenly believe that it encourages young people to engage in sexual activity. (See chapter 3.) Such a climate makes it difficult to raise financial support for sex education programs.

These obstacles, however, should not be allowed to interfere with efforts to mobilize all available forces in the protection of young people's health. Recognizing the need for cooperation among all responsible parties, the American Red Cross has made it the goal of its AIDS Prevention Program for Youth "to develop a family and school-based program that will provide junior and senior high school students with the information they need to choose behaviors that reduce the risk of contracting the AIDS/HIV virus." Its AIDS prevention program materials contain two video productions entitled *Don't Forget Sherrie* and *A Letter from Brian,* which include a student workbook, a teacher's guide, and a parent support brochure.

Clearly, the responsibilities of youth organizations have grown rapidly. Their role in compensating for diminished family power, the challenge to help poor and minority youngsters to develop into healthy and successful adults, the new urgency of addressing such threats to young people's health as teenage pregnancy and the AIDS epidemic—all place new burdens on the leadership of these groups and on their workers at every level.

Quinn stresses that leadership "whether paid or unpaid, is consistently named as a central issue, perhaps the central issue, in strengthening programs for young adolescents."

While poor and minority youngsters derive great benefits, the youth organizations' special value is that they can serve all young people across all racial and class barriers, thus bringing young people together.

Extending this perspective, Heath and McLaughlin stress that youth organizations should not simply address single issues such as pregnancy, substance abuse, or success in school but, instead, should embrace the whole person. They add that young people, particularly those who live in stressful, urban environments, want fun and recreation; but they also look for something more, "something that signals accomplishment." Apart from the fun and games, "it has to amount to something." Programs that are perceived as having been planned by adults to control young people have little chance for success. In Quinn's words, "Real success probably involves doing a better job of listening to kids and sharing the leadership with them."

The effectiveness of youth programs and their potential for supporting adolescent health and development have been amply demonstrated. What must now be faced is the necessity for sufficient funding to permit them to increase their influence in areas of poverty.

CHAPTER EIGHT

AT THE CROSSROADS

O nly hypocrites could recommend that today's young people ought to follow the example of their elders in shaping their behavior. It would be equally foolish to suggest that the problems of America's young adolescents can be viewed apart from the critical issues that confront all of American society. The spreading swamp of poverty, the greed and corruption in public and private enterprises, and the loss of faith in institutions and their leaders all conspire to undermine young people's trust in private and civic virtue. The drift toward a society that offers too much to the favored few and too little to the many inevitably raises questions among young people about the rewards of hard work and integrity. The practice of "deniability" by leaders in government and by managers of corporations allows the privileged to escape personal responsibility, not only for errors in judgment but for antisocial and even criminal behavior.

Similar problems confronted earlier generations. What is different today is the infinitely greater impact on young people because the nation's "dirty laundry" is being washed in full view of all young American adolescents. In this age of television, there is no longer a way to hide adult misbehavior from the young. When the law treats the powerful differently from the way it treats the powerless, or applies one set of rules to the rich and another to the poor, teenagers know it. We are naive if we

fail to recognize the extent to which shady, evil, and immoral adult role models shape young people's thoughts and actions.

For many adolescents, poverty is a grim reality. The fact that poverty cannot be eradicated does not excuse inaction. While the causes of poverty need to be identified, exposed, and eliminated through more effective economic and social policies, the lives of children and adolescents cannot be put on hold until these larger social, economic, and political problems are solved. Young people are entitled to health-enhancing action now. Their physical, psychological, and mental safety and well-being must be protected, not in some vague future, but today.

By the start of the twenty-first century, today's young adolescents, those aged ten to fifteen, will approach or will already have entered young adulthood. Will they have beaten the risks they now face? If they were born into poverty, will they have made it by then into the twenty-first century mainstream? Will they have been able to make the right choices in developing their bodies and minds? Will they be able to look back without deep regret to roads not taken? Will they have emerged as healthy and whole rather than as victims of the seductive and destructive appeals that play on their senses, on their fears, on their frustrations, and on their uncertainties?

MUTUAL RESPONSIBILITIES

Today's teenagers are themselves responsible for some of the answers to these questions. They are not powerless in shaping their futures and in making wise decisions about the fateful choices before them. They choose what they eat, how they treat their bodies, what harmful habits and actions to reject, and they choose how to deal with others in forming friendships and making commitments. The choices they make now will play a key role in determining their future well-being, their strength of body and mind, and, in time, their success in building sound and lasting family ties and raising healthy children.

In part, then, it is up to young adolescents to make their own choices—but only in part, for they are not immune to forces that lie beyond their control and to the environment in which they live. They need adult help.

These young people, barely past childhood, must be taught to know about their bodies and begin to understand their minds.

They must learn how their habits and actions affect their present and future physical and mental health, and beyond that, the health of the children they may bear.

They must be given a chance to master the skills they need to cope with the demands life will make on them, so that they can grasp opportunities and avoid pitfalls.

They must have the support of adults who understand adolescents and can offer constructive counsel.

They need safe and attractive places for recreation and fun.

But perhaps even more, young adolescents need a vision of a life worth living, of dreams worth aspiring to, and of possible goals to be reached. Ned O'Gorman, the poet and founder-principal of the Children's Storefront School in Harlem, said of these youngsters: "Many. . .need to be told they are important, strong, and powerful people. Society tells them quite the opposite." All young people need a firm promise that a just society awaits them—a promise of jobs with decent wages and a future that allows access to successful careers.

Instead, many young people face daunting obstacles. They are exposed to every imaginable threat to their survival.

Children of poverty and affluence alike suffer the consequences of disintegrating families, of parental neglect, and, more frequently than acknowledged or reported, of abuse and violence within the home.

Hopelessness fed by an environment of unemployment and narrowing job and career options leads to depression. Being depressed, adolescents seek escape in drugs and alcohol, compulsive eating, and, in extreme cases, suicide.

Despite these pitfalls, countless young adolescents emerge relatively unscathed from the crucial years between childhood and adulthood. Many emerge even stronger for having skirted dangers and temptations, and many more—rich and poor—emerge sound in body and mind because they have been guided and supported by understanding and caring adults at home, in school, in youth organizations, and within the community. Millions of these young adolescents know how to take advantage of the choices open to them and turn them into opportunities for healthy development.

Still, the fact that many young people succeed does not justify a disregard of those who, lacking adequate help, are likely to fail. Social and economic conditions that have created an adolescent health emergency cannot be dismissed as a normal, though deplorable, aspect of modern industrial society.

Because the unmet needs are so great, the immediate focus must be on priorities that can be tackled without delay, with appropriate funding and a high prospect of success.

Well-planned lessons in the life sciences and human biology in the upper elementary grades and middle school have been sufficiently tested to be introduced in all the nation's schools. It is an approach that, far from leading to watered-down science, could boost emphasis on and interest in the sciences, as it uses science to create an understanding of human health and health-promoting behavior. Such lessons open young eyes to a variety of risks to be avoided and opportunities to be seized, from the benefits of healthful nutrition and exercise to the dangers of drugs, alcohol, nicotine, and immature, promiscuous, and unprotected sexual activity.

School-based and school-linked health centers hold great promise for the promotion of healthy behavior and the prevention of disease. Their services should be made available to all young adolescents who need them, especially those whose families are unable to provide them. The services offered by the health centers should be all-inclusive—offering disease prevention and treatment referrals (as in cases of acute illness and injuries), and appropriate attention to the prevention of risk-prone sexual activity. They should also include counseling that

stresses the benefits of abstinence from immature and dangerous sex and encourages the planning of stable and productive,
long-lasting personal and family relationships. In response to
the realities of many young adolescents' attitudes and behavior,
such counseling should address the necessity for contraception
to prevent unwanted pregnancy and the imperative of proper
protection if sexual intercourse takes place—the use of condoms—to prevent sexually transmitted diseases.

Boys as well as girls will benefit greatly from a better understanding of the physical and psychological risks of irresponsible sexual activity. They are much more likely to make sound
choices if they gain insight about responsible sex and the responsibilities and rewards of carefully planned parenthood. If
they do become pregnant, young teenage girls deserve accurate
information about the options and consequences of abortion, of
giving birth, and of the possible course of the infant's adoption
or foster care. If they decide to have their babies, they will gain
from an open door to continued education through the combination of school and motherhood. At the same time, renewed counseling would help prevent repeat pregnancies and offer support
for a future that goes beyond parenting.

Health services must be available to all young adolescents,
regardless of their ability to pay. This calls for full health insurance coverage, including the cost of preventive services that address such adolescent problems as substance abuse, depression,
and poor nutrition.

All institutions serving young adolescents—family, neighborhood, school, community, youth organizations, churches and
synagogues, news and entertainment media, and, of course, the
private and public health services—must strive to provide
trustworthy role models. Physicians, physician assistants,
school nurses, social workers, and all other health providers
should be trained to understand adolescent problems and
behavior and to respond to them with confidence-inspiring
empathy.

Many of the existing athletics and sports practices in schools and communities cry out for reform. Coaches, as well as parents, should bring greater sensitivity and common sense to teenage activities by freeing themselves from the preoccupation with winning and concentrating instead on providing opportunities for girls as well as boys to participate fully in sports, particularly in those that can be continued and enjoyed in adult life.

Because a sense of uselessness and a lack of competence can lead to depression, young adolescents must have the opportunities to develop work skills. Schools, communities, and youth organizations should forge links with the work force and the professions, among other actions promoting after-school and summer internships and other endeavors.

It is ironic that, at the very time of so much concern about an educated work force to assure American competitiveness in international markets, business and industry have been slow to develop new programs that could reach out to adolescents to give them both a taste of what the world of work is like and a sense of the skills needed for successful employment. Other industrial countries, particularly Germany, have successfully institutionalized apprenticeships. And while some forward-looking American school administrators have sought out internships by building bridges to potential employers in public and private enterprises, much more can and should be done. Limiting teenage employment opportunities largely to unskilled fast-food service jobs does little to prepare them for a future of productive and satisfying work.

Safeguarding bodies and minds remains high on the list of priorities for the protection of adolescents' health. All persons who come in close contact with children and adolescents—teachers, health providers, police—should be alert to any signs of physical and sexual abuse, reporting them promptly to the authorities. Judges and other officers of the courts must gain better insights into the consequences of abuse so that they can act with greater sensitivity in deciding how best to protect children and adolescents from future abuse.

The easy availability and escalating use of firearms has

earned for the United States a place of shame among the Western democracies. Many teenagers today walk in the shadow of violence and under threat of bodily injury and even death. Parents, particularly but not exclusively those who live in poor neighborhoods, are in constant fear for their children's safety. Youth gangs make a mockery of claims that American cities are part of a civilized, law-abiding society.

As an interim, short-term measure for instant action, strictly patrolled safety zones should be established to permit youngsters to go to, and return from, school without fear of armed assault and without justification to carry firearms for self-protection. City officials should be expected to create these zones, but neighborhoods, with the help of school personnel, should be an integral part of the initiative. These safe areas must be cleared, not only of weapons, but also of the sale and use of drugs. Violations should be subject to quick trial and harsh penalties. The rules that govern this enterprise should be constantly reinforced by adult commitment to observing them. At the same time, schools and youth organizations must teach young people the skills and benefits of conflict resolution without the use of force.

In the long run, such limited remedies are not enough. The safety of American youths and the reclaiming of the embattled communities in which they grow up call for nothing less than the disarming of anyone not entitled, on the basis of effective registration, to own or carry a firearm. This calls for federal legislation matched by committed local enforcement. Anyone, including a parent or other relative, who makes a firearm available to a child or adolescent should be subject to severe penalties.

Although such measures are certain to incur strong political opposition, a variety of polls indicate that most Americans, particularly parents, teachers, police officers, and others alarmed by the toll of the nation's escalating violence, are now ready to support measures that will put an end to the proliferation of firearms and the mayhem of violence.

Many measures proposed to offer young adolescents a chance

to grow up safe and healthy, from school-linked health centers to gun control, will be controversial; but there is a growing consensus that the protection of young Americans' health is worthy of creative new policies, even if they entail some adult sacrifice.

In purely pragmatic terms, there is much concern whether or not today's adolescents, who will represent the United States in the next century—less than a decade away—will be able to make this nation competitive, in economics as well as in ideals. At issue is excellence in a wide variety of skills; but even skilled workers, managers, and professionals will not be able to carry the burden of competitiveness and productivity unless they are healthy in body and mind.

COST VS. SAVINGS

The cost? There is no credible or useful way to put a dollar figure on actions needed to improve and safeguard young adolescents' health. Some of it can be done without the expenditure of new money: habits and attitudes can be changed through realistic education and sound adult example. Human biology and the life sciences, conflict resolution, and the avoidance of unnecessary risks should be natural components of a relevant curriculum; so should life skills, communication skills, and critical intelligence.

Providing access to proper health care, which embraces family planning and disease prevention through the services of school-based or school-related health centers along with the extension of health insurance to cover all children and adolescents, should be part of the program of long-delayed national reforms of health care for Americans of all ages, but these measures will not come without a price tag. The preparation of, and adequate compensation for, health providers below the level of physicians also will not come cost-free.

At the heart of sound new policies to safeguard adolescent health, however, is an understanding that the ultimate effect will be one of massive savings. Good health is infinitely less costly than disease. The price to society and its taxpayers of the damage done by drugs, alcohol, and nicotine runs into hundreds of billions. Unwanted teen pregnancies and births of unhealthy at-risk babies result in unending fiscal hemorrhaging. The costs of violence in injuries, deaths, and dollars are inestimable.

The bottom line is not what those policies will cost today but, rather, how much money and misery can be saved in the long run and how much our society as a whole will benefit from the contributions made by healthy, competent young adults.

Health does not exist in isolation. To promise sound development to young people involves more than the services of health providers or devoted youth program leaders. Poverty is a threat to health. So are families in disarray, rich and poor. All forms of discrimination—race, ethnicity, and sex—breed illness of mind and heart. Satisfaction with the status quo endangers the mental and physical well-being of all whose lives cry out for change. "Do-nothing" or "do-too-little" attitudes threaten the peace of mind of the young whose lives are still unfolding.

To seek remedies for conditions that put young people at risk is costly in both resolve and money. What is needed now is a popular and political will, supported by effective reporting in the press and on television. Young adolescents at crucial crossroads in their lives must be helped now to avoid risks to their health and future well-being. To safeguard their health is not an act of charity; it is a reaffirmation of a humane society and an investment in the nation's future.

RECOMMENDATIONS

The comments that follow are based in large measure on the wide-ranging studies and publications commissioned by the Carnegie Council on Adolescent Development and on the Council's extensive discussions of the factors affecting the health of ten- to fifteen-year-old adolescents. The specific recommendations, however, are those of the author, with careful attention given to the views of the experts cited in this book.

The guiding themes have emerged from the conviction that, to be and remain healthy, adolescents need:

▲ INFORMATION: health education; life skills training, with special attention to decision making and conflict resolution; positive support by the media

▲ ACCESS TO HEALTH SERVICES: school-linked adolescent health centers; full insurance coverage including preventive health care

▲ MOTIVATION AND SUPPORT OF ADULTS: willingness and ability to use the available information and services, especially when provided by family, youth organizations, mentors, and constructive role models

▲ AN IMPROVED ENVIRONMENT: reduction of poverty; control of substance abuse and guns; more effective links to the world of work

EDUCATION

All upper elementary and middle schools should offer at least two years of health and/or life science education for all young adolescents. The life sciences should be integrated with the science curriculum.

The power of education should be harnessed to develop healthy adolescents and eliminate avoidable risks. To this end, all upper-elementary and middle schools should provide health education. School systems should introduce instruction in the life sciences, as part of the core curriculum, for at least two consecutive years between the sixth and ninth grades. The goal is to teach young adolescents to know how their bodies and minds develop and work—what strengthens them and what harms them. Such instruction will inform adolescents about the importance of proper nutrition and exercise and about the harmful consequences of substance abuse. If coupled with training in decision making, an understanding of the reproductive system can help to discourage premature and irresponsible sexual activity.

At the same time, such instruction should give added meaning and relevancy to the study of science itself.

Throughout these efforts, adolescents must be encouraged to be active participants in the search for health-giving strategies and behavior through membership in youth organizations, peer groups, and community service projects.

Key actors for implementation: health and science educators; middle school reformers; youth organization leaders.

HEALTH SERVICES

Health insurance coverage and access to health care through school-related health services must safeguard all adolescents' well-being and healthy development.

To provide access to health care, insurance coverage—private or publicly financed—must be extended to all teenagers. Such coverage must include preventive health care to forestall future problems.

School-based or school-related health centers must be established through cooperation among education, health, and social service agencies. These centers must provide easy access to those young adolescents who need such services and whose health would otherwise be jeopardized, mainly in inner cities and areas of rural poverty.

The centers should be actively involved in health promotion and disease prevention. They must care for the youngsters' dental and visual problems or, after diagnosing them, arrange for proper treatment. They must respond to injuries and acute and chronic illness, either with treatment or referral. They must recognize disabling, and often fatal, depressions and other mental health problems and take teenagers' uncertainties and fears seriously. They must look for, diagnose, and refer for treatment early signs of eating disorders and pay attention to early warnings of drug and alcohol abuse.

The centers should also deal with young adolescents' reproductive health, including sexually transmitted diseases. They should counsel about sexual behavior and its consequences, offer contraceptive advice when required, and, in the face of the growing risk of AIDS, urge the avoidance of unprotected sexual activity. While counseling should stress the moral and physical values of abstinence and postponed intercourse and child bearing, health services should be free to recommend the use of condoms and distribute them on request. In cases of teenage pregnancies, counseling should include presentation of all options, from giving birth to abortion. It should also deal effectively with the importance of prenatal care to the mother's and the baby's health.

The extension of effective health services to all young adolescents will require the simultaneous increase of the pool of specially trained health-care providers—physicians, physician assistants, nurses, psychologists, and social workers—who understand the anxieties and concerns of teenagers.

Key actors for implementation: the federal government; school boards and administrators; colleges and universities; insurers; state and local political and health officials.

MEDIA

The news and entertainment media should be enlisted to reduce violence, substance abuse, and irresponsible sexual behavior. Funding should be made available for programming that entertains while it encourages teenagers to consider the consequences of their actions.

The news and entertainment media can be of great help in influencing attitudes and behavior of children and young adolescents. Television programs are needed that entertain teenagers and, at the same time, make them think about the problems they face and the opportunities open to them.

Greater visibility and increased funding should be given to television programming that enhances rather than endangers the health and well-being of young people. That this is possible has been illustrated by the constructive approach to smoking: whereas virtually everybody was shown lighting up in old movies, cigarettes have largely disappeared from the modern screen, and no television anchor or commentator today would brandish cigarettes in the way that was something of a trademark for Edward R. Murrow.

Today, great efforts, short of censorship, should be made to purge the visual media, particularly television and rock music programs, of their orgy of mindless violence. Such reforms ought to begin with cartoons produced for young children that often make violence appear amusing.

Similarly, television programmers should be urged to eliminate irresponsible sexual behavior, and particularly unprotected sex. The industry should instead be encouraged to use its considerable constructive power to illustrate responsible sexual behavior. Educators, researchers, health providers, and other experts should work with producers and screen writers to help with these issues, especially with the risks of sexually transmitted disease and the threat of AIDS.

Advertising of alcoholic beverages and cigarettes in the media, including magazines, should cease to be directed at young people.

The media should be engaged in efforts to provide a better understanding of sound nutrition and physical exercise.

Key actors for implementation: television, film and pop music video producers, writers, and sponsors; youth experts and consultants; advertisers and advertising agencies; foundations.

THE WORLD OF WORK

Government, business, and industry must create conditions that will improve adolescents' opportunities to prepare for, and enter, the world of work. Special emphasis must be on job creation, mentoring, internships, and apprenticeships.

Young adolescents must be given an understanding and appreciation of the choices open to them in the world of work. This is particularly important for young people who grow up in an environment of unemployment and hopelessness. Raising their sights to future possibilities is crucial to their sense of self and their mental health. Without such help, their feelings of uselessness may expose them to despair, depression, early parenthood, and the delusion of escape by way of drugs and alcohol abuse.

Young adolescents must be made to feel useful and competent. They must be shown that there is a world of work beyond employment in fast-food enterprises at minimum wages or in lucrative criminal activity as recruits of drug peddlers.

There are many ways of building better connections with the world of work, including mentoring programs that engage adults from a variety of jobs, careers, and professions. These approaches must begin no later than in the middle grades. They should not be postponed, as is currently all too often the case, until the later high school years, when many students have already dropped out of school, and when those who remain have lost valuable time in thinking about the connection of their school work with their future. As a first step, the schools and other community agencies must create part-time internships during the school year and full-time internships in the summer in business and industry, hospital and other health services, senior citizen and child care centers, the schools themselves, and a variety of municipal enterprises such as the courts, the parks, public transportation, and sanitation.

All of this requires the cooperation of leaders in business, government, and labor unions. Beyond internships as an introduction to the world of work, the government, business, and industry should give serious consideration to apprenticeships as a "learn-while-you-earn" approach similar to those being used successfully in other industrial countries. Providing such opportunities could do much to make young people partners in efforts to make the United States competitive in international markets; it can bring new hope to those young people who will enter the work force without education beyond high school.

In a broader sense, the success of these crucial initiatives also depends on national, state, and local policies of job creation. Sound economic policies are imperative if young people are to be given the hope of productive and satisfying futures.

Key actors for implementation: business and industry; vocational schools; government; foundations.

CONTINUITY

Health-care providers and educators must be taught and encouraged to deal with the development of childhood and adolescence as a continuing physical, mental, and psychological process.

Anonymity is the curse of urban, industrial society. Young adolescents need close and continuing contact with caring adults to whom they can take their problems and in whose judgment they have confidence. They need the comfort and comradeship of youth organizations. *Turning Points: Preparing American Youth for the 21st Century* stressed the importance of adult mentors in the schools; *Fateful Choices: Healthy American Youth for the 21st Century* calls for the same measure of support in the field of health. Physicians and other health professionals must be trained and willing to provide personal counseling, in addition to their professional services. Personnel of school-related clinics and health centers must be available for continuing guidance, especially to adolescents whose families are not able to provide it.

Moreover, children and young people in vital stages of their physical, mental, and social development need continuity within the institutions and with the people with whom they come in contact. Just as there ought to be a better connection than now exists among those who care for infants, children, elementary school pupils, middle school students, and high schoolers, there should be continuity through personal contact and exchange of information among those who deal with the health and well-being of children and adolescents as they move from one developmental stage to the next. This calls for greater attention to such vital transitions in the training of health providers.

Key actors for implementation: physicians and other health-care providers; parents; educators; foundations.

VIOLENCE AND SAFETY

Safety zones, free of weapons and drugs, must be established around schools. Strictly enforced federal gun controls must deny children and youths access to firearms, along with a general ban on the sale and possession of unregistered guns. Youth organizations must actively compete against violent gangs for membership. Schools must stress nonviolent conflict resolution.

In the short term, drug- and weapon-free zones should be established around all schools. The goal is to assure that children and youths are able to go to and from school without fear of bodily harm. These safety zones must be under continuous scrutiny. This will require cooperation by the schools, the police, the local community and its elected representatives, and neighborhood business enterprises. Violations, such as possession of firearms, knives, and other weapons, and the sale or use of drugs, must be instantly and severely penalized through legal action. If necessary, special courts may have to be established to prevent prosecutions from becoming submerged and delayed in overcrowded court calendars.

In the long term, the existing and steadily escalating threat of violence to the health and the very lives of children and young adolescents calls for nothing less than the disarming of the American population. The proliferation of firearms, including semiautomatic weapons, is unparalleled among industrial democracies. The proper remedy is to be found in federal legislation aimed at diligently enforced gun registration, effective control of the manufacture, import, and sale of firearms, and severe penalties for violation. Penalties also should be imposed on parents and other adults who allow legitimately owned and registered firearms to fall into the hands of children and adolescents.

To be politically feasible, such legislative action must be preceded by an intense educational campaign designed to lead to an understanding that the constitutional guarantee of the right to bear arms was intended to enable the new nation to organize a citizens militia, and not to condone the indiscriminate ownership of firearms. Such an educational approach might be followed by an intensive, comprehensive public opinion poll to inform Congress about the actual popular sense about a matter of such importance to the safety of young Americans.

Youth organizations should be encouraged and funded to intensify their competition with gangs in their appeal to the loyalty of young adolescents. Instead of relying largely on police action to contain violent youth gangs, youth organizations and community groups must provide nonviolent alternatives when young people get together. These organizations can offer adolescents opportunities to be useful, to be in the company of friends, and to engage in team sports, competitive games, and community service. Since, in many dysfunctional neighborhoods, gangs often represent the only compelling structure for young people, youth organizations must be encouraged to compete with gangs for members who are searching for more enjoyable activities in the company of their peers.

Key actors for implementation: school officials; community leaders; educators; police authorities; local, state, and federal officials and legislators; the courts; youth organizations; public opinion experts; the media.

FUNDING

The health of all adolescents must be fully insured, and coverage must include illness prevention. Funding for such services as school-related health centers and life science education must be either provided or obtained through reallocation of existing funds.

The extension of health insurance to cover all young adolescents must be viewed as a vital component of the general reform of health insurance financing in general. Implementation of many other recommendations calls for added funds, but much can also be accomplished through the reallocation of existing funds. For example, while the establishment of school-related health centers will require some new federal, state, and local expenditures, many health professionals should be relocated to the schools where their clients are. The introduction of human biology and life science courses into the middle grade school curriculum may require some added funding for teacher preparation and new teaching materials, but the operating cost will be included in the ongoing school budgets for science instruction.

Setting up internships is not without cost, but much of it could be covered by business and industry as its contribution to the improvement of the future work force.

But it is also evident that the prevention of disease and health-compromising behaviors and the reduction of teenage pregnancies and the birth of at-risk babies will lead to substantial savings. Almost immediately, and certainly in the long run, these savings will greatly exceed the investments that are urgently required now. The cost of keeping an adolescent in a penal or reform institution is estimated at between $20,000 and $30,000 a year. Preventive actions, such as efforts to reduce unlawful behavior caused by substance abuse and weapons-related violence, promise large savings in money and the curtailment of human suffering.

The health of children and adolescents is inextricably linked to the health of the communities in which they live, and ultimately to the health of the nation. The costs of disease and disabilities are virtually impossible to estimate. So is the cost of poverty. The annual cost in public funds of teenage pregnancies and their aftermath is estimated by the National Research Council at between $15 billion and $18 billion. The protection of young people's physical and mental health and the prevention of disease, including depression and despair, are costly; but they are infinitely less expensive than the consequences of neglect and the resulting health-endangering behavior.

Key actors for implementation: federal, state, and local governments; health providers; school officials; business and industry; foundations.

APPENDIX

SOME MAJOR NATIONAL
YOUTH ORGANIZATIONS

AMERICAN CAMPING ASSOCIATION provides health-related programs taught by camp professionals and promotes outdoor activities, recreation, and safety and survival skills. The organization provides few national programs; its role is, rather, to support good management of camp facilities and to promote camping as part of the total educational process.

AMERICAN RED CROSS provides emergency-related services and disaster relief—health at its most basic. It also has four major areas of program priorities for young people, one of which is health promotion. Its various health and safety courses include family and community health, first aid, AIDS education, water safety, home nursing, and nutrition.

ASPIRA encourages and supports Hispanic young people in the pursuit of education. One of its initiatives, the National Health Careers Program, seeks to increase the number of Hispanic youth graduating from medical and other health professional schools. ASPIRA serves 13,000 students per year and offers the following services: recruitment, counseling, financial assistance, workshops on career choice and applications, health fairs, conferences, trips to schools, and student counseling.

BIG BROTHERS/BIG SISTERS OF AMERICA is primarily a mentoring organization and, with few exceptions, does not offer national programs as such. One exception is Empower, a national program focused on the prevention of child sexual abuse. Special health initiatives also exist at some of the local agencies and deal with child abuse prevention, service to the handicapped, substance abuse prevention, and teenage pregnancy prevention.

BOY SCOUTS OF AMERICA stresses the development of mental and physical fitness and outdoor skills. One requirement of becoming a First Class Scout is physical fitness. Badges earned by Cub Scouts include safety and swimming.

BOYS AND GIRLS CLUBS OF AMERICA has health and physical fitness among its core programs. National programs that are health related include Smart Moves, an initiative to prevent substance abuse and early sexual involvement. A demonstration project currently active in thirty-three clubs is aimed at gang prevention and intervention. The organization also sponsors national sports programs.

CAMP FIRE BOYS AND GIRLS sponsors Trail to the Great Outdoors and Trail to Knowing Me, My Family, and My Community. In addition, Camp Fire gives awards to local programs involving peer counseling that teach teens to confront the issues of drug abuse, family problems, and suicide: a drug abuse prevention program (Up with Health/Down with Drugs) that hires teenagers to work with younger children after school, specifically on how to resist using drugs; a suicide prevention program (sail); and a program that teaches teens how to deal with stress (smart). Camp Fire Boys and Girls was awarded a contract from the U.S. Office for Substance Abuse Prevention to develop a model community-based drug abuse prevention program.

COSSMHO (National Coalition of Hispanic Health and Human Service Organizations) was founded by mental health professionals to improve community-based mental health services for Hispanics. In 1978, the organization expanded to include health and human service organizations and professionals. Members currently include community-based health and mental health organizations, social service providers, practitioners and officials in the fields of public health, nursing, social work, psychology, and youth services, and research programs and educational institutions. Its programs include health research, health promotion, and disease prevention and the education and training of health-care providers. Existing demonstration projects include AIDS education, alcohol and drug prevention, gang and drug abuse prevention, and inhalant abuse prevention.

4-H CLUBS encourages young people to complete projects of their choice and includes classes in nutrition, diet, and health. Through these projects, young people learn about daily food needs, nutrition, health, fitness, food preservation, and food preparation. The 4-H Expanded Food and Nutrition Education Program is a nationwide project that helps economically disadvantaged youth acquire skills and knowledge in nutrition education and improve their diets. Drug abuse prevention is also taught through health projects and food and fitness projects.

GIRL SCOUTS OF THE USA stresses personal well-being and fitness. Activities focus on physical and mental health including nutrition and exercise, interpersonal relationships, the home, safety, work and leisure, and consumer awareness. The organization publishes a series of booklets called *Contemporary Issues*, which address current topics including preventing teenage pregnancy, growing up female, preventing youth suicide, preventing child abuse, and preventing substance abuse.

GIRLS INCORPORATED offers a broad scope of activities in every area of life management pertinent to girls. Health-related programs include health and physical fitness, adolescent pregnancy, drug education, and sexual abuse prevention. National pro-

grams include Preventing Adolescent Pregnancy; Friendly
Peersuasion—peer education about the dangers of alcohol, tobacco, and drug abuse; Sporting Chance—to increase interest
and participation in athletics; AIDS education; Kidability—skills
in avoiding sexual abuse; Girl Power/Health Power—personal
responsibility for health care in the areas of nutrition, physical
fitness, reproductive health, and substance abuse; and Teen
Connections—physical fitness workshops, health fairs, opportunities for community action around health issues, and case
management for at-risk adolescents.

NAACP (National Association for the Advancement of Colored
People), although not primarily a youth organization, has a
Youth and College Division that serves older adolescents and
young adults. The NAACP's health programs for youth include
antidrug and teenage pregnancy workshops.

NATIONAL NETWORK OF RUNAWAY AND YOUTH SERVICES is a
network of approximately 900 organizations that serve runaway, homeless, and other at-risk children. Basically, these organizations offer safe shelter and counseling to young people.
Two national programs are (1) Youth-Reaching-Youth, a peer
counseling program that discourages drug abuse; and (2) an
AIDS prevention program called Safe Choices.

NATIONAL URBAN LEAGUE has national programs that address
adolescent pregnancy prevention and parenting, teaching adolescent male responsibility as a component, as well as drug, tobacco, and alcohol prevention, through a project called Time to
Be Me: Looking at My Future.

SALVATION ARMY includes the Girls Guards and Adventure
Corps, which offer projects in health. The organization also offers programs for pregnant teens and teen mothers and provides safe shelter, food, and counseling. One of its national programs, Bridging the Gap Between Youth and Community

Services, teaches adolescents to use community resources, including health services.

YMCA OF THE USA is a charitable organization dedicated to building healthy minds, bodies, and spirits. Among the five priorities of its youth programs is improving personal health. Its sports programs include swimming, basketball, baseball, softball, fitness, martial arts, and substance abuse prevention.

YWCA OF THE USA promotes health, sports participation, and fitness for women and girls. "Health care" is one of the YWCA's five public policy priorities. Its programs include health instruction, teen pregnancy prevention, family life education, self-esteem enhancement, parenting, and nutrition. The YWCA also offers special programs for teens about pregnancy prevention, parenting, and sexuality. One of its national programs is Peer Approach Counseling by Teens, which trains adolescents to teach peers about human sexuality.

Abramson, Jill. "Selling Moderation: Alcohol Industry Is at Forefront of Efforts to Curb Drunkenness." *Wall Street Journal* (May 21, 1991).

Alexander, Elizabeth A., Ken J. Kallail, Jeanne P. Burdsal, and David L. Ege. "Multifactorial Causes of Adolescent Driver Accidents: Investigation of Time as a Major Variable." *Journal of Adolescent Health Care* 11 (1990): 413–17.

Anderson, John E., Laura Kann, Deborah Holtzman, Susan Arday, Ben Truman, and Lloyd Kolbe. "HIV/AIDS Knowledge and Sexual Behavior Among High School Students." *Family Planning Perspectives* 22 (1990): 252–55.

Barrett, Paul M. "Epidemic: Killing of 15-Year-Old Is Part of Escalation of Murder by Juveniles." *Wall Street Journal* (March 25, 1991).

Blum., Robert W. "Global Trends in Adolescent Health." *Journal of the American Medical Association* 265 (1991): 2711–19.

Blum, Robert W., and Linda H. Bearinger. "Knowledge and Attitudes of Health Professionals Toward Adolescent Health Care." *Journal of Adolescent Health Care* 11 (1990): 289–94.

Cohen, Stu, and Cynthia Lang. "Application of Principles of Community-Based Programs." Background paper prepared for the Forum on Youth Violence in Minority Communities: Setting the Agenda for Prevention, Atlanta, December 10–12,

1990. Cosponsored by Centers for Disease Control and the Minority Health Professions Foundation with the Morehouse School of Medicine.

Cohen, Stu, and Renée Wilson-Brewer. "Violence Prevention for Young Adolescents: The State of the Art of Program Evaluation." Paper prepared by the Education Development Center, Inc., for the conference Violence Prevention for Young Adolescents, Washington, D.C., July 12–13, 1990. Supported by Carnegie Corporation of New York.

Cortines, Ramón C. "A Practitioner's Perspective on the Interrelationship of the Health and Education of Children." Paper presented at a meeting of the National Health/Education Consortium, Washington, D.C., May 29, 1990.

Dryfoos, Joy G. *Adolescents at Risk: Prevalence and Prevention.* New York: Oxford University Press, 1990.

Earls, Felton, Robert B. Cairns, and James Mercy. "The Control of Violence and the Promotion of Non-Violence in Adolescence." In *Adolescent Health Promotion,* edited by Susan G. Millstein, Anne C. Petersen, and Elena O. Nightingale (in preparation). New York: Oxford University Press, 1992.

Elliott, Delbert S. "Health Enhancing and Health Compromising Lifestyles." In *Adolescent Health Promotion,* edited by Susan G. Millstein, Anne C. Petersen, and Elena O. Nightingale (in preparation). New York: Oxford University Press, 1992.

Feldman, S. Shirley, and Glen R. Elliott, eds. *At the Threshold: The Developing Adolescent.* Cambridge: Harvard University Press, 1990.

Fransen, Vivian E., ed. *Proceedings: AIDS Prevention and Services Workshop, February 15–16, 1990, Washington, D.C.* Princeton: Robert Wood Johnson Foundation Communications Office, June 1990.

Friedman, Lawrence S., Brenda Johnson, and Allan S. Brett. "Evaluation of Substance-Abusing Adolescents by Primary Care Physicians." *Journal of Adolescent Health Care* 11 (1990): 227–30.

Goldsmith, Marsha F. "School-based Health Clinics Provide Essential Care." *Journal of the American Medical Association* 265 (1991): 2458–60.

Hamburg, David A., *Today's Children: Creating a Future for a Generation in Crisis.* New York: Times Books, 1992.

Heath, Shirley Brice, and Milbrey Wallin McLaughlin. "Community Organizations as Family: Endeavors That Engage and Support Adolescents." *Phi Delta Kappan* 72 (1991): 623–27.

Hechinger, Grace. *How to Raise a Street-Smart Child: The Complete Parent's Guide to Safety on the Street and at Home.* New York: Facts on File Publications, 1984.

Hendrix, Kate, and Patricia J. Molloy. "Interventions in Early Childhood." Background paper prepared for the Forum on Youth Violence in Minority Communities: Setting the Agenda for Prevention, Atlanta, December 10–12, 1990. Cosponsored by Centers for Disease Control and the Minority Health Professions Foundation with the Morehouse School of Medicine.

Henshaw, Stanley K., Asta M. Kenney, Debra Somberg, and Jennifer Van Vort. *Teenage Pregnancy in the United States: The Scope of the Problem and State Responses.* New York: Alan Guttmacher Institute, 1989.

Hernandez, Jeanne T., and Frank J. Smith. "Inconsistencies and Misperceptions Putting College Students at Risk of HIV Infection." *Journal of Adolescent Health Care* 11 (1990): 295–97.

Hingson, Ralph W., Lee Strunin, Beth M. Berlin, and Timothy Heeren. "Beliefs About AIDS, Use of Alcohol and Drugs, and Unprotected Sex Among Massachusetts Adolescents." *American Journal of Public Health* 80, no. 3 (1990): 295–99.

Hofferth, Sandra L., and Cheryl D. Hayes, eds. *Risking the Future: Adolescent Sexuality, Pregnancy, and Childbearing. Working Papers.* Washington: National Academy Press, 1987.

Ianni, Francis A. J. *The Search for Structure: A Report on*

American Youth Today. New York: Free Press, Macmillan, 1989.

Kellermann, Arthur L., Roberta K. Lee, James A. Mercy, and Joyce Banton. "The Epidemiologic Basis for the Prevention of Firearm Injuries." *Annual Review of Public Health* 12 (1991): 17–40.

Killen, Joel D., C. Barr Taylor, Michael J. Telch, Keith E. Saylor, David J. Maron, and Thomas N. Robinson. "Evidence for an Alcohol-Stress Link Among Normal Weight Adolescents Reporting Purging Behavior." *International Journal of Eating Disorders* 6 (1987): 349–56.

Klerman, Lorraine V. "Health and the Social Environment: The Influence of Poverty." In *Adolescent Health Promotion,* edited by Susan G. Millstein, Anne C. Petersen, and Elena O. Nightingale (in preparation). New York: Oxford University Press, 1992.

Kotlowitz, Alex. *There Are No Children Here: The Story of Two Boys Growing Up in the Other America.* New York: Doubleday, 1991.

Krugman, Richard D. "Child Abuse and Neglect: Critical First Steps in Response to a National Emergency: The Report of the U.S. Advisory Board on Child Abuse and Neglect." In *Caring for the Uninsured and Underinsured: A Compendium from the Specialty Journals of the American Medical Association.* Chicago: American Medical Association, 1991.

Kunins, Hillary, and Allan Rosenfield. "Abortion: A Legal and Public Health Perspective." *Annual Review of Public Health* 12 (1991): 361–82.

Lear, Julia Graham, Hope Burness Gleicher, Anne St. Germaine, and Philip J. Porter. "Re-organizing Health Care for Adolescents: The Experience of the School-based Adolescent Health Care Program." Work supported by grants from the Robert Wood Johnson Foundation. Unpublished manuscript.

Leventhal, Howard, and Patricia Keeshan. "Promoting Healthy

Alternatives to Substance Abuse." In *Adolescent Health Promotion*, edited by Susan G. Millstein, Anne C. Petersen, and Elena O. Nightingale (in preparation). New York: Oxford University Press, 1992.

MacNeil/Lehrer Productions, WNET, and WETA (coproducers). "MacNeil/Lehrer NewsHour" [Television program]. "Conversation: Murder in America." Show no. 4006, April 8, 1991. Overland Park, Kans.: "Strictly Business." Transcript.

——. "MacNeil/Lehrer NewsHour" [Television program]. "Conversation: Murder in America." Show no. 4007, April 9, 1991. Overland Park, Kans.: "Strictly Business." Transcript.

——. "MacNeil/Lehrer NewsHour" [Television program]. "Series: Murder in America." Show no. 4009, April 11, 1991. Overland Park, Kans.: "Strictly Business." Transcript.

——. "MacNeil/Lehrer NewsHour" [Television program]. "Series: Murder in America." Show no. 4010, April 12, 1991. Overland Park, Kans.: "Strictly Business." Transcript.

——. "MacNeil/Lehrer NewsHour" [Television program]. "Focus: Disarming Proposal." Show no. 4054, June 13, 1991. Overland Park, Kans.: "Strictly Business." Transcript.

Marshall, Ray. *The State of Families: Losing Direction—Families, Human Resource Development, and Economic Performance*. Milwaukee: Family Service America, 1991.

Marx, Fern. "After School Programs for Low-Income Young Adolescents: Overview and Program Profiles." 1989. Working Paper no. 194. Study made possible by a grant from the Children's Defense Fund. Unpublished manuscript.

Maurer, Harold M. "The Growing Neglect of American Children." In *Caring for the Uninsured and Underinsured: A Compendium from the Specialty Journals of the American Medical Association*. Chicago: American Medical Association, 1991.

Medrich, Elliott A., with the assistance of Carolyn Marzke. "Young Adolescents and Discretionary Time Use: The Nature of Life Outside School." February 1991. Prepared for the Carnegie Council on Adolescent Development Task

Force on Youth Development and Community Programs. Unpublished manuscript.

Meredith, Carol N., and Johanna T. Dwyer. "Nutrition and Exercise: Effects on Adolescent Health." *Annual Review of Public Health* 12 (1991): 309–33.

Millstein, Susan G. "A View of Health From the Adolescent's Perspective." In *Adolescent Health Promotion*, edited by Susan G. Millstein, Anne C. Petersen, and Elena O. Nightingale (in preparation). New York: Oxford University Press, 1992.

Millstein, Susan G., and Iris F. Litt. "Adolescent Health." In *At the Threshold: The Developing Adolescent*, edited by S. Shirley Feldman and Glen R. Elliott, 431–56. Cambridge: Harvard University Press, 1990.

Millstein, Susan G., Anne C. Petersen, and Elena O. Nightingale, eds. *Adolescent Health Promotion*. (In preparation). New York: Oxford University Press, 1992.

National Commission on Children. *Beyond Rhetoric: A New American Agenda for Children and Families*. Washington: National Commission on Children, 1991.

National Commission on the Role of the School and the Community in Improving Adolescent Health. *Code Blue: Uniting for Healthier Youth*. Alexandria, Va.: National Association of State Boards of Education; Chicago: American Medical Association, 1990.

Nightingale, Elena O., and Lisa Wolverton. "Adolescent Rolelessness in Modern Society." Washington: Carnegie Council on Adolescent Development, 1988.

Northrop, Daphne, and Kim Hamrick. "Weapons and Minority Youth Violence." Background paper prepared for the Forum on Youth Violence in Minority Communities: Setting the Agenda for Prevention, Atlanta, December 10–12, 1990. Cosponsored by Centers for Disease Control and the Minority Health Professions Foundation with the Morehouse School of Medicine.

Northrop, Daphne, Beth Jacklin, Stu Cohen, and Renée Wilson-

Brewer. "Violence Prevention Strategies Targeted Towards High-Risk Minority Youth." Background paper prepared for the Forum on Youth Violence in Minority Communities: Setting the Agenda for Prevention, Atlanta, December 10–12, 1990. Cosponsored by Centers for Disease Control and the Minority Health Professions Foundation with the Morehouse School of Medicine.

O'Donnell, Lydia, Stu Cohen, and Alice Hausman. "The Evaluation of Community-based Violence Prevention Programs." Background paper prepared for the Forum on Youth Violence in Minority Communities: Setting the Agenda for Prevention, Atlanta, December 10–12, 1990. Cosponsored by Centers for Disease Control and the Minority Health Professions Foundation with the Morehouse School of Medicine.

Office on Smoking and Health and the Division of Adolescent and School Health, National Center for Chronic Disease Prevention and Health Promotion, Centers for Disease Control. "Tobacco Use Among High School Students—United States, 1990." *Morbidity and Mortality Weekly Report* 40, no. 36 (September 13, 1991): 617–19.

Palla, Barbara, and Iris F. Litt. "Medical Complications of Eating Disorders in Adolescents." *Pediatrics* 81 (1988): 613–23.

Parks, Peggy L., and Edward K. Arndt. "Differences Between Adolescent and Adult Mothers of Infants." *Journal of Adolescent Health Care* 11 (1990): 248–53.

Pendergrast, Robert A., Jr., "Skateboard Injuries in Children and Adolescents." *Journal of Adolescent Health Care* 11 (1990): 408–12.

Perry, Cheryl L., Steven H. Kelder, and Kelli Komro. "The Social World of Adolescents: Family, Peers, Schools, and Community." In *Adolescent Health Promotion*, edited by Susan G. Millstein, Anne C. Petersen, and Elena O. Nightingale (in preparation). New York: Oxford University Press, 1992.

Pittman, Karen J., with Marlene Wright. "A Rationale for Enhancing the Role of the Non-School Voluntary Sector in

Youth Development." February 1991. Prepared for the Carnegie Council on Adolescent Development Task Force on Youth Development and Community Programs. Unpublished manuscript.

Quinn, Jane. "Natural Allies: Youth Organizations as Partners in AIDS Education." In *The AIDS Challenge: Prevention Education for Young People*, edited by Marcia Quackenbush. Santa Cruz, Calif.: Network Publications, 1988.

————. "Programs for Young Adolescents—A National Perspective." Presentation at the Forum for the Initiation of PRIDE: Policy, Research, and Intervention for Development in Early Adolescence, Pennsylvania State University College of Health and Human Development, February 28, 1991.

————. "Youth Organizations: A Valuable Sex Education Resource." In *Sexuality Education: A Resource Book*, edited by Carol Cassell and Pamela Wilson. Hamden, Conn.: Garland Publishing, 1989.

Richards, Maryse H., Regina C. Casper, and Reed Larson. "Weight and Eating Concerns Among Pre- and Young Adolescent Boys and Girls." *Journal of Adolescent Health Care* 11 (1990): 203–9.

Richmond, George. *The Micro-Society School: A Real World in Miniature*. New York: Harper and Row, 1973.

Rickert, Vaughn I., Anita Gottlieb, and M. Susan Jay. "A Comparison of Three Clinic-based AIDS Education Programs on Female Adolescents' Knowledge, Attitudes, and Behavior." *Journal of Adolescent Health Care* 11 (1990): 298–303.

————. "Effects of a Peer-counseled AIDS Education Program on Knowledge, Attitudes, and Satisfaction of Adolescents." *Journal of Adolescent Health Care* 12 (1991): 38–43.

Sallis, James F. "Promoting Healthful Diet and Physical Activity." In *Adolescent Health Promotion*, edited by Susan G. Millstein, Anne C. Petersen, and Elena O. Nightingale (in preparation). New York: Oxford University Press, 1992.

Schorr, Lisbeth B., with Daniel Schorr. *Within Our Reach:*

Breaking the Cycle of Disadvantage. New York: Anchor Press, Doubleday, 1988.

Seawell, Mary Ann. "Like Gangs, Successful Inner-City Organizations View Youth as Asset, Not Liability, Study Determines." *Campus Report* (August 28, 1991): 1, 8–9.

Seefeldt, Vern, Martha Ewing, and Stephan Walk. "An Overview of Youth Sports Programs in the United States." (Executive Summary and Manuscript.) 1991. Commissioned for the Carnegie Council on Adolescent Development Task Force on Youth Development and Community Programs. Unpublished manuscript.

Smith, Christen. "Overview of Youth Recreation Programs in the United States." May 1991 and August 1991 drafts. Prepared for the Carnegie Council on Adolescent Development Task Force on Youth Development and Community Programs. Unpublished manuscript.

Smith, Peggy B., Maxine L. Weinman, Teresa C. Johnson, and Raymond B. Wait. "Incentives and Their Influence on Appointment Compliance in a Teenage Family-Planning Clinic." *Journal of Adolescent Health Care* 11 (1990): 445–48.

Stone, Rebecca. *Adolescents and Abortion: Choice in Crisis.* Washington: Center for Population Options, 1990.

Strain, James E., "The American Academy of Pediatrics Response to the Growing Health Needs of Children." In *Caring for the Uninsured and Underinsured: A Compendium from the Specialty Journals of the American Medical Association.* Chicago: American Medical Association, 1991.

Task Force on Education of Young Adolescents. *Turning Points: Preparing American Youth for the 21st Century.* Washington: Carnegie Corporation of New York, Carnegie Council on Adolescent Development, 1989.

U.S. Congress Office of Technology Assessment. *Adolescent Health.* Vol. 1, *Summary and Policy Options.* OTA-H-468. Washington: U.S. Government Printing Office, April 1991.

U.S. Department of Health and Human Services, Office of Inspector General. *Youth and Alcohol: A National Survey—Do They Know What They're Drinking?* OEI-09–91–00653. Washington: U.S. Government Printing Office, June 1991.

————. *Youth and Alcohol: Drinking Habits, Access, and Knowledge.* Washington: U.S. Government Printing Office, June 1991.

U.S. Department of Health and Human Services, Public Health Service. *Healthy People 2000: National Health Promotion and Disease Prevention Objectives.* (PHS) 91–50212. Washington: U.S. Government Printing Office, 1991.

U.S. General Accounting Office. *Drug Education: School-based Programs Seen as Useful but Impact Unknown.* GAO/HRD-91–27. Report to the Chairman, Committee on Governmental Affairs, U.S. Senate. Washington: U.S. Government Printing Office, November 1990.

Weisman, Jonathan. "New Study May Provide First Evidence of the Effectiveness of Sex Education." *Education Week* (January 23, 1991).

Wilson-Brewer, Renée, and Beth Jacklin. "Violence Prevention Strategies Targeted at the General Population of Minority Youth." Background paper prepared for the Forum on Youth Violence in Minority Communities: Setting the Agenda for Prevention, Atlanta, December 10–12, 1990. Cosponsored by Centers for Disease Control and the Minority Health Professions Foundation with the Morehouse School of Medicine.

Wilson-Brewer, Renée, Stu Cohen, Lydia O'Donnell, and Irene F. Goodman. "Violence Prevention for Young Adolescents: A Survey of the State of the Art." Revised version of the working paper prepared by the Education Development Center, Inc., for the conference Violence Prevention for Young Adolescents, Washington, D.C., July 12–13, 1990. Supported by Carnegie Corporation of New York.

Witkin, Gordon, with Stephen J. Hedges, Constance Johnson, Monika Guttman, Laura Thomas, and Anne Moncreiff Arrarte. "Kids Who Kill." *U.S. News & World Report*, April 8, 1991, 26–32.

Women's Guide to Stanford Collective. *A Women's Guide to Stanford*. Fifth Edition. Stanford University.

Zinsmeister, Karl. "Growing Up Scared." *The Atlantic*, June 1990, 49–66.

INDEX

COVER PHOTOGRAPHY

Harold Feinstein, *Children of War*

INTERIOR PHOTOGRAPHY

Ed Keating, *New York Times:* page 20
Lee Zaichick, *Education Week:* page 47
Stephen Shames, Matrix International, Inc.: page 71
Paul Fusco, Magnum Photos, Inc.: page 108
Eugene Richards, Magnum Photos, Inc.: page 141
Daniel Hall, age 9, Shooting Back, Inc.: page 172
Benjamin Tice Smith: page 188
Harold Feinstein, *Children of War:* page 207

BOOK DESIGN AND TYPOGRAPHY

Meadows & Wiser, Washington, D.C.